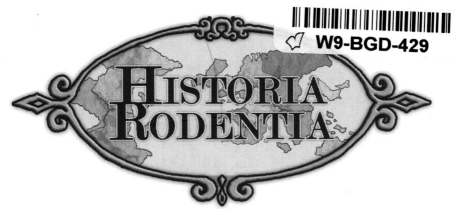

HISTORIA RODENTIA

A Brushfire supplement for the Legend roleplaying system.

Edition 1.0

CONTENTS

WRITTEN BY
Matthew Whitehouse
Emily Fontana

WITH ASSISTANCE FROM
Nick Hedge
Daniel Fokine
Pedro Panzardi
Joe Saloom
Wes Taylor
Will Warren

ART BY
Heath Foley
Noah Page
James Kaiser II

Brief Overview of *Historia Rodentia*

Historia Rodentia is a roleplaying supplement for the *Legend* roleplaying system. It provides background and mechanics for playing in the *Brushfire* universe, a setting where animals live and war like humans of the 19th Century. Unlike standard roleplaying settings that focus on a small band destroying monsters and exploring dungeons, *Historia Rodentia* sets Adventurers on the world stage, navigating political intrigue and fighting wars with thousands of lives at stake. The flavor of the world mixes equal parts real history with animal adventure stories like the *Redwall* series, *The Secret of NIMH*, or *American Tail*. The setting is appropriate for Adventurers of all ages but an enjoyment of history and parody is a great asset.

Changes from Legend

Very little of the core mechanics have been changed from *Legend* to *Historia Rodentia* but a number of new features are included in this book:

- The different species that an Adventurer can be, requiring falling within a certain size bracket to 'take' that species during Adventurer Creation.

- Magic is unknown in *Historia Rodentia* except to frauds and charlatans. To replace magic, Tactical Abilities, Politics and Exemplarism are detailed in this book.

- Organizations expand upon cults and guilds, covering major political, military, religious and scientific institutions in the *Brushfire* universe.

- A focus on firearms is also a change from *Legend* as weapons technology from the 19th century is very different from the exotic black powder weapons of the medieval age.

- Four new advanced skills have also been added, two each paired to Politics and Exemplarism. These skills play off the military and political scope of *Historia Rodentia* helping Adventurers command soldiers and call in favors from their allies.

ADVENTURER CREATION

Adventurer Creation follows the same basic rules as in the *Legend Core Rulebook*. You may use either the roll or point buy method to determine stats.

Species Template SIZ

To be a member of a species, the Adventurer must fall within the appropriate SIZ range. If by rolling for your Characteristics your SIZ fell outside the range for a species you really wanted to play, discuss with the GM to move around a characteristic point or two, to get into the SIZ range. It should be noted that these numbers are abstracts and that a creature that is a Tiny SIZ 12 will not be the same Height and Weight as a Large SIZ 12.

Tiny - 6-12 SIZ	Very Large - 16-22 SIZ
Small - 8-14 SIZ	Huge - 20-26 SIZ
Medium - 10-16 SIZ	Giant - 26-32 SIZ
Large - 12-18 SIZ	

To determine the size of creatures in relation to Meters, consider 'Small' to be about 1 Meter tall with each bracket increasing this amount by half a meter. The jump from Huge to Giant is also 1 Meter.

Species Templates use 50 of the free Skill Points as given in the Adventurer Creation section of the *Legend Core Rulebook*. The Remaining 200 points are free to be used after selecting a Species.

Animals that have Large Tails are able to use them in combat as an additional unarmed attack, or to equip Tail Only weapons, armor, or other devices. Animals listed as having Prehensile Tails also may use them to grip objects.

Hit Locations

Two basic Hit Location Tables are used for *Historia Rodentia*. Each Species Template indicates which table it uses. A Large Tail has the same Hit Points as a Leg, while a Small Tail has half the hit points of a leg.

Hit Location - Large Tail		Hit Location - Small Tail	
R.Leg: 1-3	L.Leg: 4-6	R.Leg: 1-3	L.Leg: 4-6
Tail: 7-8	Abdomen: 9-11	Tail: 7	Abdomen: 8-10
Chest: 12-14	R.Arm: 15-16	Chest: 11-14	R.Arm: 15-16
L.Arm: 17-18	Head: 19-20	L.Arm: 17-18	Head: 19-20

Species of Eutheria

If any Advanced Skills are redundantly provided by Species, Background, or Profession, the Skill gains an additional +10% bonus, or in the case of Lore/Craft may be taken again for another applicable type.

The Empire of Aquitar

Badger

Any Badger of the Melinae, Mellivorinae, or Taxidiinae Subfamilies
SIZ - Large | Small Tail
Average Lifespan - 90 Years
Common Skills - +10% Brawn, +5% Resilience, +5% Unarmed
Advanced Skills - +5% Craft(Carpentry), +5% Craft(Choice)
Trait - Bestial Claws - Badger claws are made to tear through almost anything. Even where tools are available, Badgers are as likely to use their own claws as cutting or carving instruments. For every 20% Unarmed Skill, a Badger deals +1 damage Unarmed, or wearing Claw weapons. They also take halved penalties for not having the appropriate tools for Craft (Carpenter) and similar cutting or carving crafts.

Gopher/Marmot

Geomys breviceps or Marmota marmota
SIZ - Small (Gopher) or Medium (Marmot) | Small Tail
Average Lifespan - 80 Years
Common Skills - +5% Evaluate, +10% First Aid
Advanced Skills - +10% Mechanisms, +5% Healing
Trait - Hoarders - Gophers and Marmots love items, anything new and useful they try to hold onto. This pairs well with their usual professions which require dozens of tools or medical supplies. Gopher and Marmot maximum ENC is STR+SIZ x2 and they only suffer -10% penalties for being overloaded.

Mole

Any Mole of the Talpidae Family
SIZ - Small | Small Tail
Average Lifespan - 80 Years
Common Skills - +10% Influence, +5% Insight, +5% Perception, +10% Persistence
Advanced Skills - Engineering, Oratory

MONGOOSE
GOPHER

Trait - Digger - Moles thrive in the underground. Groups of nomadic moles can live underground in low light and low oxygen for years on end. This lifestyle gives Moles the ability to see up to 5 meters in front of them in complete darkness. They also may hold their breath for CONx10 Seconds and add +10% to Resilience rolls for Asphyxiation.

Mongoose/Weasel
Any Mongoose of the Herpestidae Family or Weasel of the Mustela Genus
SIZ - Medium | Large Tail
Average Lifespan - 80 Years
Common Skills - +10% Athletics, +10% Evade, +5% Perception
Advanced Skills - +5% Acrobatics, Gambling
Trait - Quick - Mongoose and Weasels show little fear against enemies larger than them or with a longer reach. When closing or disengaging, Weasels and Mongoose add +20% to their Dodge if their opponent attempts to attack them. They also have a +5 Strike Rank.

Shrew
Any Shrew of the Soricidae Family
SIZ - Small | Small Tail
Average Lifespan - 80 Years
Common Skills - +5% Culture(Own), +10% Influence, +5% Ride
Advanced Skills - Commerce, +10% Courtesy
Trait - Echolocation - The only flightless mammals to bear this ability, Shrews continue to operate perfectly in the dark. Shrews receive no penalties based on darkness as long as they are able to speak.

BADGER   WEASEL   MARMOT
  MOLE   ShREW

The Civitan Trade Alliance

Capybara

Hydrochoerus hydrochaeris
SIZ - Large | Small Tail
Average Lifespan - 90 Years
Common Skills - +15% Swim, +10% Brawn, +5% Influence
Advanced Skills - Boating, Shiphandling
Trait - Water Hog - At home in the water and on land, Capybara make the perfect Merchant Marines. When swimming, Capybara move normal at their full Movement rate. When in Combat they can Charge or Sprint in water.

Chipmunk

Any chipmunk of the Tamias, Eutamias, or Neotamias genera
SIZ - Tiny | Large Tail
Average Lifespan - 70 Years
Common Skills - +5% Drive, +5% Evaluate,
Advanced Skills - +10% Engineering, +10% Mechanisms
Trait - Chipping - Some chipmunks live their lives surrounded by cannons, machine guns and other engines of war. Luckily, their natural ability to 'chip' out commands allows them to communicate even in the loudest of situations, ignoring penalties from noise on skills involving speaking. Chipping also counts as an additional language that only Chipmunks may speak but others can learn.
Logical Mind - So focused are the keen minds and skillful claws of the Chipmunk that any engineering work costs only 75% of the normal budget (does not stack with critical).

City Mouse

Any mouse of the Mus Genus
SIZ - Tiny | Large Tail
Average Lifespan - 50 Years
Common Skills - +5% Athletics, +5% Evade, +5% Evaluate, +5% Sleight, +10% Stealth
Advanced Skills - Commerce, Streetwise
Trait - Abacus - Mice are extremely good with numbers. They can give an exact count of a collection of items, money, or living beings with only a 1% error. They also gain 5% extra money from sales and rewards.

Jumping Mouse

Any jumping mouse of the Dipodidae Family.
SIZ - Tiny | Large Tail
Average Lifespan - 70 Years
Common Skills - +10% Athletics, +10% Evade
Advanced Skills - +10% Acrobatics, Survival
Trait - Fleet - Jumping Mice originate in the mountains high on the island of Brisica, such life has given them the ability to move +2 meters during Combat Actions on flat ground and +10% to Athletics for Jumping.

Sardan Pika

Prolagus sardus
SIZ - Medium | Small Tail
Average Lifespan - 60 Years
Common Skills - +10% Evade, +10% Perception, +10% Stealth
Advanced Skills - Survival, Track
Trait - Fleet - Sardan Pikas live in harsh jungles and pride themselves on their tracking skills. Keeping up with their prey results in a Movement bonus of +2 meters during Combat Actions on flat ground and +10% to Athletics for Jumping.

SARDAN PIKA   CAPYBARA   CHIPMUNK
CITY MOUSE   JUMPING MOUSE

Sultanate of Scyzantium

Agamid
Or any member of the Family: Agamidae.
SIZ - Medium | Large Tail
Average Lifespan - 150 Years
Common Skills - +5% Evaluate, +10% Influence, +5% Insight, +5% Persistence
Advanced Skills - +5% Courtesy, Oratory
Trait - Scaly - Many lizards have extremely tough hides, Agamids among them. Their scaly skin provides an innate 2 armor to all Hit Locations but do not incur an Armor Penalty from these Armor Points.
Alternate Traits (Draco Agamids)
Slightly Scaly - Many lizards have extremely tough hides, Draco are not among them. Their slightly scaly skin provides an innate 1 armor to all Hit Locations but do not incur an Armor Penalty from these Armor Points.
Glider - Agamids of the Draco Genus are accustomed to gliding for short distances, +20% to Athletics for Jumping.

Anole
SIZ - Tiny | Large Tail
Average Lifespan - 60 Years
Common Skills - +10% Athletics, +10% Drive, +5% Swim
Advanced Skills - Engineering, +5% Mechanisms
Trait - Autonomy - Anoles have an extremely effective regeneration ability, able to even regenerate its tail if dismembered. Anoles have a natural healing rate of 1 HP per 12 Hours and may make a Resilience check the day after receiving a major wound to their Tail to heal it naturally.
Adept Rider - Anoles suffer 10% less penalty for any Ride Checks, including when riding unfamiliar mounts, or riding through rough terrain or water.

Chameleon
Or any member of Family: Chamaeleonidae
SIZ - Small | Large Tail
Average Lifespan - 90 Years
Common Skills - +10% Athletics, +10% Stealth, +10% Sleight, +10% Evade
Advanced Skills - Streetwise
Trait - Prehensile Tail - In addition to attacking unarmed with its Tail, a chameleon can use its flexible tail to hold or grip objects, like a third hand.
Slightly Scaly - Many lizards have extremely tough hides, Chameleons are not among them. Their slightly scaly skin provides an innate 1 armor to all Hit Locations but do not incur an Armor Penalty from these Armor Points.

Monitor Lizard

Or any Member of the Genus: Varanus
SIZ - Large | Large Tail
Average Lifespan - 110 Years
Common Skills - +10% Brawn, +5% Drive, +5% Ride, +10% Influence
Advanced Skills - Courtesy, Oratory
Trait - Scaly - Many lizards have extremely tough hides, Monitors among them. Their scaly skin provides an innate 2 armor to all Hit Locations but do not incur an Armor Penalty from these Armor Points.

Sand Lizard

Or any member of the Genus: Lacerta
SIZ - Large | Large Tail
Average Lifespan - 150 Years
Common Skills - +10% Brawn, +10% Resilience,
Advanced Skills - +5% Streetwise, +5% Survival
Trait - Scaly - Many lizards have extremely tough hides, Sand Lizards among them. Their scaly skin provides an innate 2 armor to all Hit Locations but do not incur an Armor Penalty from these Armor Points.

Gecko

Gekko gecko
SIZ - Tiny | Large Tail
Average Lifespan - 80 Years
Common Skills - +10% Athletics, +10% Perception, +10% Ride
Advanced Skills - Survival, Track
Trait - Wall Walking - The pads on a gecko's hands and feet allow it to walk on walls and ceilings at half Movement rate.

MONITOR LIZARD   AGAMID   SAND LIZARD
CHAMELEON   GECKO   ANOLE

The Vandalands

Gerbil

Any Gerbil of the Gerbillinae Subfamily
SIZ - Tiny | Large Tail
Average Lifespan - 80 Years
Common Skills - +5% Drive, +5% Evaluate, +5% First Aid
Advanced Skills - +10% Engineering, +5% Mechanisms
Trait - Fleet - Gerbils originate in the cool steppes of the Vandalands, such life has given them the ability to move +2 meters during Combat Actions on flat ground and +10% to Athletics for Jumping.

Hamster

Any Hamster of the Cricetinae Subfamily
SIZ - Small | Small Tail
Average Lifespan - 60 Years
Common Skills - +15% Brawn, +5% Resilience
Advanced Skills - +10% Survival, Track
Trait - Territorial Rage - Hamsters fight to the death, preferably someone else's, over their small parcels of land in the northlands. Once per day as a free action, a Hamster may invoke Berserk as detailed in the *Legend Core Rulebook* on themselves. During berserk they may not call for Favors but may use Battlefield Awareness. Heroic Command rolls have a -20% while a Hamster is berserking.

hAMSTER   ShREW   GERBIL

Hedgehog

Any Hedgehog of the Erinaceidae Family
SIZ - Small | Small Tail
Average Lifespan - 80 Years
Common Skills - +5% Culture(Own), +10% Insight, +10% Ride,
Advanced Skills - Courtesy, +5% Oratory
Trait - Spiny - The quills of a Hedgehog protect it from attack when it curls up to defend itself. Instead of Evading or Parrying attacks at Medium or Short Reach, the Hedgehog may deal one point of damage ignoring armor to the attacker if they successfully hit the Hedgehog. This damage is dealt to the limb that attacks the Hedgehog.

Shrew

Any Shrew of the Soricidae Family
SIZ - Small | Small Tail
Average Lifespan - 80 Years
Common Skills - +5% Culture(Own), +10% Influence, +5% Ride
Advanced Skills - Commerce, +10% Courtesy
Trait - Echolocation - The only flightless mammals to bear this ability, Shrews continue to operate perfectly in the dark. Shrews receive no penalties based on darkness as long as they are able to speak.

Rat

Any Rat of the Rattus Genus

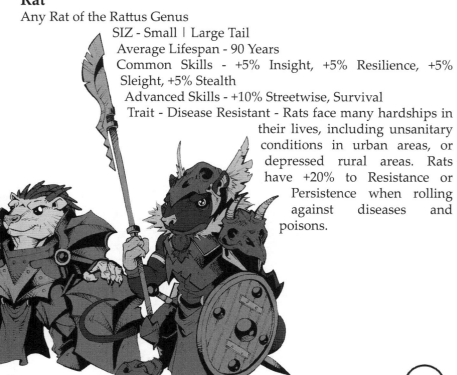

SIZ - Small | Large Tail
Average Lifespan - 90 Years
Common Skills - +5% Insight, +5% Resilience, +5% Sleight, +5% Stealth
Advanced Skills - +10% Streetwise, Survival
Trait - Disease Resistant - Rats face many hardships in their lives, including unsanitary conditions in urban areas, or depressed rural areas. Rats have +20% to Resistance or Persistence when rolling against diseases and poisons.

World Mechanics

Starting Money

The standard currency in *Historia Rodentia* is the Civitan Murin. It is an international coinage and it does not use decimalization. (200 copper murin: 20 silver murin: 1 gold murin) When referring to Murin without a metal quality, gold is the automatic assumption. For adventuring purposes, Adventurers use Civitan Murins for trade. The enterprising nature of the Trade Alliance has allowed its citizens to use the murin as a de facto currency in many places around the world. Other coinage are used only within their countries and colonies.

Coinage of other Nations
Aquitaran Aquin - Decimalized
1 Aquin Cent = ~2.4 Copper Murin
1 Aquin = ~24 Silver Murin

Vandal Thaler - Non-fractional single unit currency.
1 Thaler = ~50 Copper Murin

Scyzantine Asper/Solidus - Bimetal currency
50 Silver Asper = 1 Gold Solidus
1 Silver Asper = ~2 Silver Murin.

Time

On the Rodentian calendar a year is 10 months and covers 290 Days. A Day spans 30 hours, averaging 20 hours of light for most of the year and 15 hours during the winter months.

Cultures

The Region or Lifestyle your Adventurer lives in; these are Limited by National Background and provide skills and starting money. Each Background provides +50% to Language (Native), based on your Nation. (Aquitaran, Vandal, Civitan, or Scyzantine)

Nomadic - Vandalands or Scyzantium

While not the expert Riders that people of the march are, the nomadic peoples of Scyzantium and Vandalands roam the untamed wildernesses of their respective nations. The extremely harsh environments create hardy people that have learned to survive with little support system over the centuries.

Skills: Same as core *Legend*, except includes +10% Ride automatically.
Choice: +10% Brawn, Drive, or Swim.
Starting Money: Same as core *Legend*.

Barbarian - Vandalands

While the majority of Vandals have civilized since the fall of the Rodentian Empire, several tribes still retain their old cultures. Living along the Fjords of the northern coast, Hamsters are the most endemic Barbarians of the Vandalands but smaller groups of Rats and Gerbils also reside high in the mountains.

Skills: Same as core *Legend*
Starting Money: Same as core *Legend*

Urban (Upper Class) - Any

The Upper crust of Eutherian societies have struggled to retain their grip in the last centuries, from revolutions, to riots, the Upper Class of most nations see themselves as the last bastion of culture and civilization. Such views are what lead to their initial problems but this has not stopped them from cultivating an air of superiority in the posher regions of most cities.

Common - +30% to Culture(Own) and Lore(Regional); +20% to Influence, Evaluate
Combat Style - +10% to 2: 2H Spear, Bow, Crossbow, Dagger, Polearm, Rapier, Spear and Shield, Sword and Shield, Firearms
Advanced Skills - Courtesy; 2 Choices: Ride, Art, Boating, Commerce, Craft(any), Engineering, Healing, Language(any), Mechanisms, Oratory, Shiphandling, Lore(any)
Starting Money - 4D6 x 30 Silver Murin

Urban (Lower Class) - Any

The down trodden, the working man, while the Upper class immediately take officer ranks and laze about, the Lower class must trudge the trenches or work in factories. Such harsh realities have encouraged a basic survival instinct in highly populated urban areas. In recent years the plight of the lower class has lessened, especially in Aquitar and Civitas.

Common - +30% to Culture(Own) and Lore(Regional); +10% Sleight, Stealth, Evaluate, Insight

Combat Style - +10% Unarmed, +10% to 2: 1H Hammer, 2H Hammer, Dagger, Rapier, Sword and Shield, Bow, Crossbow, Firearms, Spear and Shield, Polearm, Unarmed.

Advanced Skills - Streetwise; 2 Choices: Commerce, Craft(any), Gambling, Lore(any), Boating, Shiphandling, Play Instrument

Starting Money - 4D6 x 10 Silver Murin

Marches - Any

The borderlands between countries is no place for a civilian, people who live in the Marches are warriors first, protecting their nation's borders from incursion. The peoples of the Marches are experts in cavalry and general Birdsmanship or Turtlesmanship, trekking the large expanses from town to town, sleeping in a different bed every night.

Common - +30% to Culture(Own) and Lore(Regional); +20% to Ride and Athletics

Combat Style - +15% to 2: Firearms, Spear and Shield, Crossbow, Sword and Shield, Polearm

Advanced Skills - Track; 1 Choice: Craft(any), Language(any), Lore(any), Survival, Healing, Disguise

Starting Money - 4D6 x 30 Silver Murin

Colonial - Civitas or Aquitar

The far flung continents of North and South Vespuccia were ripe for conquering 200 years ago. Now the tide of colonists has slowed but much of the new world is still untamed. Colonists still identify with their homelands but also develop unique cultures in their new homes. Holding a wide range of skills is paramount to survival 3,000 miles away from civilization.

Common - +30% to Culture(Own) and Lore(Regional); +10% First Aid, Resilience and Swim

Combat Style - Unarmed +10%, +10% to 1: Firearms, Bow, Crossbow, Sword and Shield, Axe and Shield, 2H Axe, Dagger, Hammer and Shield, 2H Hammer

Advanced Skills - Survival, Lore(New World); 3 Choices: Boating, Shiphandling, Track, Language(any), Healing, Engineering, Craft(any)

Starting Money - 4D6 x 20 Silver Murin

Naval - Civitas, Aquitar or Scyzantium

The backbone of any colonial empire, the sailors of Civitas and Aquitar make long trips across the Lemurian Ocean, bringing supplies to colonists and fighting piracy. The navy of Scyzantium patrols the smaller Bharatese Sea protecting fishing vessels and trading with neighboring nations. Regardless of country of origin, sailors enjoy a life of adventure, exploration and scurvy.

Common - +15% to Culture(Own) and Lore(Regional); +10% Athletics, Brawn, Perception, Swim

Combat Style - +10% to 2: Firearms, Bow, Crossbow, 2H Axe, Axe, 2H Sword, Sword, Spear, Polearm, Rapier, Dagger

Advanced Skills - Culture(any) +15%, Lore(any region); 2 Choices: Boating, Shiphandling, Streetwise, Survival, Play Instrument, Language(any), Gambling, Craft(any)

Starting Money - 4D6 x 20 Silver Murin

Professions

After selecting your background, you may choose an eligible profession based on your background. If a profession from the *Legend Core Rulebook* is not listed here, its not possible to take in a *Historia Rodentia* campaign. Many of the professions from Legend have not been changed. Those that have been changed detail everything the profession provides below.

Acrobat - Barbarian, Urban (Lower Class), Marches, Naval
Animal Trainer - Any
Bard - Any
Blacksmith - Barbarian, Urban (Lower Class), Colonial
Champion - Any
Influence +5%, Athletics OR Brawn OR Riding +5%
+10% to any 2 Combat Styles appropriate to your Background
Battlefield Awareness, Heroic Command
Chemist - Urban(Lower Class), Marches, Nomad
Evaluate +10%, First Aid +10%, Perception +10%
Craft(Chemistry), Lore(Chemistry)
Courtier - Urban(Upper Class)
Influence 5%, Lore(Regional) 5%, Perception 5%, Sleight or Dance 5%
Lore(Organization), Duty(Organization)
Select ONE Advanced Skill - Courtesy, Lore(Art), Lore(Heraldry), Lore(Philosophy), Play Instrument
Craftsman - Any
Diplomat - Urban(Upper Class), Marches, Colonial
Culture(Own) +10%, Influence +10%, Perception +10%
Lore(Organization), Duty(Organization)
Explorer - Any

Farmer - Marches, Colonial

Hunter - Marches, Colonial, Nomad, Barbarian

Noble - Urban(Upper Class), Marches, Naval
Influence +10%, Persistence +10%
Sword Combat Style
Select ONE Advanced Skill
Select ONE Politics or Exemplarism Skill

Mercenary - Any
+10% to TWO - Athletics, Evade, Driving, Evaluate, Reslience, Riding, Unarmed
+10% to any 2 Combat Styles appropriate to your Background
Battlefield Awareness

Merchant - Any

Miner - Urban(Lower Class), Marches, Colonial

Revolutionary - Urban(Lower Class), Marches, Naval, Colonial
Perception +10%, Sleight +5%, Stealth +5%
Oratory
Select 2 Political or Exemplarism skills

Physician - Urban(Upper Class), Urban(Lower Class), Marches, Colonial

Priest - Any
Influence +15%, Lore(Regional) +5%, Persistence +10%
Lore(Religious Organization), Duty(Religious Organization)

Sailor - Naval, Urban(Lower Class)

Scholar - Urban(Upper Class)

Soldier - Any
Select Two: Athletics 5%, Brawn 5%, Evade 5%, Resilience 5%
+10% to One Combat Style
Battlefield Awareness, Heroic Command

Spy - Any

Tactician - Urban(Upper Class), Marches, Naval
Influence +5%, Perception +10%, Ride +5%
Shiphandling +5%, Insight +5%
Duty(Organization), Heroic Command

Thief - Any

Tracker - Barbarian, Nomad, Marches, Colonial

Weapons Designer - Urban(Upper Class), Urban(Lower Class)
Evaluate +10%, Perception +5%, Drive +5%
Engineering, Mechanisms, Craft(Any)

Woodsman - Barbarian, Nomad, Marches, Colonial

Magic in Historia Rodentia

Magic does not exist in the world of *Historia Rodentia*, there are many mysteries as yet unsolved in the world but with a trained eye any could be explained with science. Adventurers in *Historia Rodentia* do not have access to Common, Spirit, Sorcery, or Divine Magic. These are replaced by Politics and Exemplarisim, which can be found in Chapters 2 & 3.

POW

As magic does not exist in *Historia Rodentia*, Power takes a different aspect. This Characteristic represents an Adventurer's clout and sway over others, especially relating to their position of Power in their nation. Adventurers with high POW usually hold important stations within the government or at least have many people who owe them favors. This is not directly related to their CHA, as even nasty people can rule or attain power. Few Adventurers ever attain a POW of 21, only great conquerors or rulers of empires can exceed this value. If your POW is ever reduced to zero, you do not die but have lost any influence in the world, likely exiled from your homeland, or thrown into prison as a traitor.

Dedicated POW

Dedicating yourself to an organization reduces your overall influence on outsiders but helps raise you through the ranks and gain unique opportunities from your comrades.

Starting Equipment

In *Historia Rodentia* new Adventurers gain a set of 'Freebie' Equipment depending on the type of Campaign.

Common Campaign
- One Weapon relevant to your weapon skills and culture
- A week's worth of food and water
- Some personal mementos, good luck charms/talismans, or similar
- Clothes and a set of spares.

Military Campaigns
- Up to two Weapons relevant to your job.
- Uniform (Provides 1 AR to all Hit Locations)
- Off Duty clothes.
- A week's worth of food and water.
- Some personal mementos, good luck charms/talismans, or similar

Politics

Intrigue and Politics go hand in hand. Politicians must be aware of threats on a grand scale and act accordingly. Knowledge of the inner workings of their own Organizations can help a Politician realize what foes and allies they have. By serving the needs of their group and therefore their nation, Politicians gain Favors from their leaders. By calling in these favors Politicians can gain extra troops for battle, new weapons, supplies, learn valuable information, or even utilize the unique features of their Organization.

Lore (Specific Organization)
(INT+POW)

Knowledge of the inner workings of an organization, its purpose, past victories and failures and operating within the system allows the Politician to call upon Favors they have gained through their service. On a critical success, the Favor is not lost but its effects still occur. On a fumble, your contact has snubbed you, the favor is lost and does not occur.

Duty (Specific Organization or Person)
(CHA+Dedicated POW)

Duty is paramount to military, religious and even some civilian organizations. By following the rules of the order and furthering the cause of the Organization, new favors open up to the Politician and old favors can be used again. Critical successes of the Duty skill recovers all used Favors, a fumbled roll results in no gained Favors and returning to the Headquarters or other important facility of the Organization can help return your standing.

Duty Improvement
1D10+1 - Complete a mission on behalf of the organization
1D6 - Fail a mission on behalf of the organization
1D4+1 - Complete a mission on behalf of the Nation
1D2 - Fail a mission on behalf of the nation
1 per POW - Dedicate POW to Duty(Organization)
1 per event - Upholding the rules and cause of the organization in extreme circumstances.

Calling in Favors
Favors are not immediate, if your fortress is being over run, it is too late to send a message requesting reinforcements. Favors can be called upon in two basic ways: Request or Supplication. Requesting a Favor allows you to send messages to your allies within your Organization to send you aid. The time required for such aid to be rendered depends entirely on your distance from help. The GM must decide how long a runner or rider would take to send for help and where the help would be coming from. Supplication brings the Adventurer into the halls of the Organization to beg for assistance. In such situations where the Politician has come before the council, leader, or the Ally who provides the favor, the Politician can add the critical range of the Influence skill to their Favor roll. To call in a Favor, the Adventurer must select a Favor and make a Lore (Organization) roll. This ensures that your favor abides by the rules of the Organization and that your Ally feels comfortable providing such aid.

The number of favors you may have is equal to your Dedicated POW.

Favor Render Time

Requesting the Reinforcements Favor may take two days for a message to be sent to your Ally when you are protecting a border town. But an army barracks is only a days ride from your position. Your Ally knows people in the Nation's army and sends word to the barracks to make haste to your position. Rendering the Favor took a total of 3 days for 100 Riflemice to come to your aid.

Regaining Favors

Once a favor has been called, your Ally will be unwilling to render such aid again. Only so many battalions can be sent to help you before the Organization may get suspicious. Each rank within an organization provides alternate means to regain favors.

Private - May regain favors by Supplication by making a Duty roll before an Organizational Commander. Failure requires you to try again the following week.

Sergeant - May regain favors by Supplication by making a Duty roll before an Organizational Commander. Failure requires you to try again the following day.

Officer - May regain favors by Request by making a Duty roll and sending a message by courier. Failure results in the courier being eaten by a badger and the Politician must Supplicate to a Commander.

Commander - May regain favors by Request by making a Duty roll adding Influence's critical range. Failure requires you to try a Request the following day, a fumble requires Supplication before the supreme heads of the Organization.

Pool of Favors

As you gain favors, you do not gain specific favors but gain a use from a specific category. Favor categories include: Army Intelligence, Troop Reinforcements, Extra Supplies and Political Pull. Each time you use a favor from a category your total in it is reduced. Regaining favors raises the number in a specific category by one.

Increasing Favor Count

Favors are fulfilled by members of the Organization the Adventurer belongs to. This provides excellent roleplaying opportunities for the GM to design events or even adventures around. Rather than gaining individual favors, an Adventurer increases the total of one category of Favors. Specific Favors within each category have their own Rank requirement and may also have other restrictions upon them. To gain additional favor, select a category and spend an Improvement Roll and make a Lore (Organization) roll, adding the critical range of Influence. A successful roll provides an additional Favor in the category and possibly a new Ally. If the category did not previously have a Favor count, the GM should definitely add a new Ally from the

Organization (a newly created one, or a previous person of interest) to the Adventurer's set of allies. This person is the one who will provide aid when a favor is called upon. Each Adventurer starts with a total number of favors equal to their rank in an organization at Adventurer Creation. The player should pick which category the favors belong to and they need not all belong to the same category.

Increasing Favor Count Chart

Current Rank	Minimum Location
Private	Headquarters
Sergeant	Any Office
Officer/Commander	Request

Each Favor Count costs one more improvement roll than the previous count in the category. The first Favor costs one improvement, the second costs two and so on.

Favor Traits & Descriptions

Rank - Minimum Organization rank to call upon the favor.
Time - The minimum time it takes for aid to be rendered. Add additional time if a Request is sent and if the Adventurer is far from help.

Commander Favors

When you have more control of the organization, you can call in amazing favors. Any Favors that require Commander Rank, use all of your Favors in that category.

Favor List

The favors listed here are merely examples, in other situations you may request different favors from your organization. The GM should determine the nature of these favors and what quality of favors are equivalent to your current rank.

Army Intelligence

This is a very abstract category, the exact effectiveness of each favor should be determined by the GM.

Lay of the Land - Private - Time: 5 Hours
Provides detailed information on the geography of an area.

Enemy Numbers - Sergeant - Time: 5 Hours
Provides detailed information on enemy troops in an area.

Bombardment - Officer - 10 Min when at War, 2 Days when at peace
An armada of ships along the coast, or a battery of cannons near your position, take aim and barrage an area of your choice. This attack may begin at a preset time, or may be signaled with a flare.

National Secrets - Commander - Time: 1 Day

A spy has snuck into the most vital areas of the enemy's high command and brought back key information to a future attack, a flaw in a weapon's design, or the time an important position will be undefended.

Troop Reinforcements

Favors can call a variety of soldiers to help your missions. As these troops may have other places to be, make a Duty roll with increasing difficulty at the end of each day, to see if they return to their posts in the morning. They will automatically leave when your current mission is finished.

Irregulars - Private - Time: 1 Day

Between 10 and 20 Irregular Troops come to your aid to finish your current mission. These troops are ill-equipped and should use the underling rules.

Trained Troops - Sergeant - Time: 1 Day

Between 5 and 10 Troops come to your aid to finish your current mission. These troops are well equipped but should use the General HP rules.

Cavalry - Officer - Time: 12 Hours

Between 3 and 6 Cavalry soldiers come to your aid to finish your current mission. These troops are equipped with appropriate mounts for their faction and should use normal HP rules.

Specialists - Officer - Time: Varies

Each organization has its own Specialists, view the details in the Companion section of the Exemplarism Chapter.

Hero & Warband - Commander - Time: 3 Days

A person of interest from your organization and their own personal retinue(if applicable) come to your aid. These soldiers will only come to your aid on missions for the organization.

Extra Supplies

The exact amount of supplies should be directly based on how well the Politician rolled. Any supplies should be appropriate for how advanced or the scale of the game being played. Small, character centric games should only provide a few supplies. Campaigns that follow epic wars across Eutheria, should provide supplies to feed an army. While the minimum time for Supplies is listed rather low for a political favor, the GM should adjust this time not only based on distance but the overall position of the organization or nation. A country on the losing side of a war cannot muster supplies as readily to cover all fronts. Supplies may also come out of an Adventurers pay from their organization if their requests begin to cut into the budget.

Food and Medical Supplies - Private - Time: 1 Hour
Provides supplies for basic survival: Rations, first aid kits and clean water or beer.

Ammo and Basic Weapons - Sergeant - Time: 1 Hour
Provides enough weapons and ammo to arm a small civilian populous. These weapons are far from high quality but the ammo is decent enough for your own use.

Special Weapons - Officer - Time: 5 Hours
Provides weapons unique to your nation and other higher quality weapons. Only a few weapons are provided in this favor and no ammo is provided.

Prototype Weapon - Commander - Time: 1 Day
Each Nation has its own weapons development firm and thus, its own unique prototype weapons. Refer to Venture Company for Civitas, Federwerk Industries for Vandalands, Undermining Inc. for Aquitar and Fortress Adwaita for Scyzantium. These organizations may be willing to part with one of their rare designs for your use. Can only be used on a mission for your nation, one of the development organizations, or your own organization.

Political Pull

Your contacts can also use their own political strength to provide favors to you. There is no minimum time for Political Pull, the only time required is the time to send messages to the contact and to their liaisons within the government. Political Pull refers to your contact's Duty skill score. It is appropriate to either progress the contact as the Politician develops or increases rank in the Organization, or create a new contact at higher ranks. The over all effectiveness of these Favors is based on the Duty skill being at high enough level to be of worth.

A Good Word - Private
Provides the critical range of your contact's Duty to a specified Influence roll. Good Words only affect Military and Organizational Rank, Crimes committed and similar bureaucracy.

Border Crossing - Sergeant
Your contact is able to get you papers that allow you into a restricted area, past a security check point, or allow free movement in other nations. Each use of Border Crossing provides it for a specific use and Disguise rolls must be made to prove the papers are genuine. Such rolls add the contact's Duty critical range to your score.

Trust - Officer
Your contact has faith in you, even if the rest of the world does not. If the Politician has been framed, or other forms of intrigue have pitted enemies at home against them, using this favor ensures all of your contacts within your organization are still on your side and won't give you up. The contact's Duty critical range counts as a penalty to

Insight or Perception for those seeking out the Politician. If the GM truly wishes for an inside traitor, then the Contact at least warns the Politician to possible threats.

Change Mind - Commander

Forces a politician from your nation to side with the Adventurer against their better judgement. Shades of Grey morality may be involved in the coercing of the politician. No rolls are required here but your contact may be placed in an awkward position, resulting in criminal charges against you or him. In extreme uses Change Mind may require Duty rolls for the contact or the Politician and further 'adventuring' through the criminal system.

Exemplarism

Exemplarism does not work like a magic from *Legend*, as the name alludes, Exemplars lead by Example. Their actions in war time bring soldiers under their sway and keep all of them alive to return home. Exemplars are leaders that guide from the front. They stand at the cusp of the trenches calling for a charge and rush across the battlefield at the Vanguard of their troops. Feats of Exemplarism bind fellow soldiers to an Exemplar, either swayed by his overall charisma, or saved by his actions in the line of duty, Companion Soldiers will follow an Exemplar into hell itself.

Battlefield Awareness

(POW+CON)

An Exemplar has become attuned to the sounds and sights of combat. Even the slightest changes in their surroundings due to unseen threats, flag a subconscious warning. In situations where Opposed rolls are required against Stealth, Disguise, or Sleight with an Insight or Perception Roll, add Battlefield Awareness' critical range to your score. If such a roll is fumbled, stress of war has caused the Exemplar's senses to fail them and additional Awareness rolls cannot be made that day. On a success, if the Exemplar is in combat, he may immediately use an available Combat Action out of Strike Rank order. On a critical success he may make a free Combat Action and use a regularly available Combat Action immediately. Once an Awareness test has been made, additional rolls cannot be made during that combat.

Heroic Command

(POW+CHA)

Compelling others on the battlefield can swing entire wars in your favor, Heroic Command can be used to coerce a shaken comrade to keep fighting through their own fear, or provide its critical range to mass-battle rolls.

Using Exemplarism

By saving a soldier's life, compelling them to battle via the Heroic Command skill, or through another action the GM sees fit, a soldier may become duty-bound to the Exemplar. If the Exemplar saves the soldier's life during the Combat Actions available through Battlefield Awareness, add the critical range to the Heroic Command roll. A successful Heroic Command roll causes the friendly soldier to become duty-bound.

Squad Mate

Every Exemplar went through training along side squad mates. As those not cut out for the Organization dropped out, those that remained became closer and more trusting of each other. An Exemplar has one Squad Mate that they would trust with their life beyond the normal realms of brothers in arms. The GM and Exemplar should work together to design a Squad Mate with a personality and background of their own. Unlike other NPC allies a Squad Mate has a number of innate bonuses.

The Squad Mate has Battlefield Awareness and Heroic Command equal to half the Exemplar's score. Your Squad Mate can use Battlefield Awareness to sense incoming dangers and take appropriate action.

A Squad Mate does not have to be paid for their services and remain with the Exemplar for as long as his Organization's rules are upheld. Squad Mates have access to all the Heroic Abilities that an Exemplar does, as long as they fulfill all requirements other than Legend Points and Rank requirement.

The Exemplar's Improvement rolls may be applied to the Squad Mate. Additionally, the Squad Mate gains 1 Improvement roll (no modifiers allowed) when Improvement rolls are doled out.

Squad Mate Statistics

Your Squad Mate can be derived from any of the templates listed in this chapter or from the Specialist template to an Organization to which you belong.

Commanding Your Squad Mate

During Combat, the Exemplar may use a free action to give basic commands to a Squad Mate such as 'flank them' or 'give me covering fire'. Beyond these basic commands, a Squad Mate is controlled by the GM. In instances where the Exemplar wishes to give a command that is either foolhardy, or especially dangerous, the Exemplar must make a Heroic Command test to sway his Squad Mate. If the test is failed, the Squad Mate hesitates and follows either a previous command, or does nothing. On a fumble, the Squad Mate's trust in your orders is shaken and 5% is removed from their own Heroic Command. On a critical success, the Squad Mate's trust is cemented and the order followed exactly, with that, the Squad Mate's Heroic Command is increased by 5% (up to the original value).

Alienating your Squad Mate

Too many wild orders, or violations of an Organization's rules may result in your Squad Mate abandoning you. This may come in different forms. The Squad Mate may just go AWOL, or in extreme circumstances, report your actions to your superiors. How exactly your Squad Mate leaves is up to the GM and the severity of your actions. There is a safety net however. Your Squad Mate's own Heroic Command score represents both his own command ability and his trust in yours. As bad commands are given, or your own actions violate the rules of your Organization, the GM should deduct 5% from the Squad Mate's Heroic Command. When the value reaches zero, he has had enough and cannot abide by your command style any longer. Critical successes on commands and actions that enforce the rules or ideals of your Organization can strengthen trust and return 5% at a time up to the Squad Mate's original Heroic Command score.

Duty-Bound Companions

In addition to your Squad Mate, Those who see your feats of heroism can also become companions, assisting you in combat and following your commands. You can have a number of soldiers under you command this way based on your current rank in an organization

Private: ¼ of CHA
Sergeant: ½ of CHA
Officer: ¾ of CHA
Commander: All of CHA

Soldiers of Higher Rank or higher POW will not follow your commands. Soldiers beyond the number allowed by your Rank and CHA may still follow your commands but are not duty-bound to.

Recruiting Companions

While anyone can hire mercenaries, or have soldiers placed at their command by superior officers, these are transitory companions, who will leave once the pay dries up, or the mission is completed. Duty-Bound Companions will continue to follow you on further adventures. By using Battlefield Awareness to a save a soldiers life, or risking your own to complete a mission, onlookers can be swayed by your Heroic Command score into continuing to serve under you. When such events occur, the GM can select nearby allies that may have been swayed by such feats and make a Persistence roll against the Exemplar's Heroic Command. If the Exemplar wins the roll, the soldier becomes swayed. On a critical success for the Exemplar, or a Fumble for the soldier, the potential companion is automatically duty bound. On a fumble for the Exemplar, or a Critical success for the Soldier, the potential companion may instead report the Exemplar to his superiors for stupidly risking his own life for glory. Such results may incur a penalty to the Exemplar's Heroic Command for a period of time.

These companions, unless they previously had statistics written up for them, should count as Underlings as listed in the *Legend Core Rulebook*. Companions should not be the turning point of a battle except in large numbers.

Swayed Companions

People that are swayed by your actions are not necessarily going to follow you down a path of destruction; at least, not right away. Swayed Companions may stick around in awe of your abilities but may leave if their previous obligations call them elsewhere. Swayed companions can be turned to full Duty-Bound companions in a number of ways.

Save their lives AGAIN - A Heroic Success on Swayed companions make them Duty-Bound

Persuade them to join you - Opposed Influence against Persistence can bring the Companion around to fully agree with your actions.

Arrange for their transfer - If the companion belongs to your organization and you are of a higher rank, you can appeal to your superiors to place this person at your command, such a transfer would be made with the Politics system, adding the Heroic Command critical range to the Request or Supplication. A Transfer order would count towards any Favor Type. GM's choice as to which should be deducted.

Duty-Bound Companions

Now that you have a small army at your side, an Exemplar can give Duty-Bound companions orders in the same fashion as a Squad Mate. Companions however do not have any of the extra benefits that a Squad Mate has. They do have a Heroic Command value equal to ¼ the Exemplar's Heroic Command and bad orders or actions can cause them to abandon you in the same fashion as your Squad Mate.

Organizational Companions

Companions can also be granted to you by the organization you belong to. These companions are automatically duty-bound, as they have been placed at your command by your superiors. These companions are available for selection of the Exemplar, able to be handpicked for the tasks ahead. Any type of Companion, as listed below may be gained in this fashion but Specialist Companions can be taken from the same list as Squad Mates.

Private - No Organizational Companions
Sergeant - ¼ of Total Companions
Officer - ½ of Total Companions
Commander - ¾ of Total Companions

Types of Companions

Here are a basic list of universal Companions that can be gained. Each provides a unique trait which can often be compounded with additional companions of the same type, or complimented by different companions.

Scouts - Light ranged companions, that are experts at tracking and revealing enemy positions.

Sniper - Expert marksmen, Snipers are less likely to trigger Battlefield Awareness.

Combat Engineer - Explosives expert, able to destroy structures and plan tunnels and trenches.

Shock Trooper - Melee fighters, their brutishness helps them survive multiple ranged attacks to close in and break enemy ranks.

Specialists - Each Organization has their own Specialists with unique equipment and traits.

Squad Mates have 200 Skill Points to spend. No skill can exceed 75% at creation. At creation these points may only be spent on the skills listed for the archetype.

Companions have 100 Skill Points to spend. No skill can exceed 50% at creation. At creation these points may only be spent on the skills listed for the archetype.

Selecting a Species gives the average of the SIZ range provided on the template. Other than whether the animal has a tail, no other bonuses are provided from a Species Template.

Scout Companion

STR	3D6	Common Skills - Athletics, Evade, Perception, Stealth, Swim
CON	3D6	
DEX	2D6+6	Advanced Skills - Acrobatics, Survival, Track
SIZ	Species	Combat Actions - 2
INT	2D6+6	Movement - 10m
POW	1D6+6	Strike Rank - +10
CHA	3D6	Weapon Types (2 choices from List) +5% to One Combat Style

Bow, Crossbow, Dagger, Sword, Rifle, Pistol

Scouting - Can perform Lay of the Land and Enemy Numbers as a single favor using minimum time. Scout must pass an opposed stealth test against any opponents he tries to observe or is caught during his scouting mission.

Sniper Companion

STR	3D6	Common Skills - Athletics, Perception, Stealth, Swim
CON	3D6	Advanced Skills - Disguise, Survival, Streetwise
DEX	2D6+6	Combat Actions - 3
SIZ	Species	Movement - 8m
INT	2D6+6	Strike Rank - +10
POW	1D6+6	Weapon Types(2 choices from List) +10% to one
CHA	3D6	Ranged Combat style
		Bow, Crossbow, Dagger, Sword, Rifle

Hideaway - Snipers that have made a successful stealth or disguise roll from beyond 25 meters, cannot be detected via Battlefield Awareness, until their first attack in combat.

Combat Engineer Companion

STR	3D6	Common Skills - First Aid, Perception
CON	3D6	Advanced Skills - Engineering, Mechanisms,
DEX	3D6	Combat Actions - 2
SIZ	Species	Movement - 6m
INT	2D6+6	Strike Rank - +5
POW	1D6+6	Weapon Types(1 choice from List) +10% to one Combat
CHA	3D6	Style.
		Pistol, Rifle, Sword, Dagger, Hammer, Axe

Sapper - Explosives can be purposefully detonated by the Combat Engineer without rolling for a random detonation time. Engineering's Critical range can also be added to Combat Style(Firearms) or Combat Style(Artillery).

Shock Trooper Companion

STR	2D6+6	Common Skills - Athletics, Brawn, Evade, Unarmed
CON	2D6+6	Advanced Skills - None
DEX	3D6	Combat Actions - 3
SIZ	Species	Movement - 8m
INT	2D6+6	Strike Rank - +10
POW	1D6+6	Weapon Types (2 choices from List) +20% to one Melee
CHA	3D6	Combat Style and Unarmed
		Any 1H Melee weapon, Any 2H Melee Weapon, Any

Melee Weapon and Shield

Blitz - Shock Troopers have Double the normal HP for Underlings or General HP NPCs and gain +20% Evade for the remainder of a round when they Charge or Sprint.

Specialist Companion

STR	2D6+5	Common Skills - See Organization
CON	2D6+5	Advanced Skills - See Organization
DEX	2D6+5	Combat Actions - 3
SIZ	Species	Movement - 8m
INT	2D6+5	Strike Rank - +10
POW	1D6+6	Weapon Types - See Organization
CHA	2D6+5	Skilled - A Specialist is considered to be at officer rank
		of an organization. They have each organizational

skill at a minimum of 80% (Or higher to meet minimum requirements for an officer of that organization) and are Equipped as befitting their organization.

TACTICAL ACTIONS

Tactical Abilities are special abilities, similar to Heroic Abilities from the *Legend Core Rulebook* but more readily available to Adventurers in *Historia Rodentia*.

They come in two types: Tactical Actions and Tactical Passives. Tactical Actions work similar to Magic or Heroic abilities, in that a player invokes the action as opposed to passives which simply are 'on' all the time.

As magic does not exist in *Historia Rodentia*, Tactical Points replace Magic Points and are derived from Int + Dex / 2, rather than POW. Performing these abilities requires mental and physical quickness. While reaching zero Tactical Points does not result in unconsciousness, it does result in a level of Fatigue. Tactical Points are regained in the same fashion as Magic Points (except up to Int + Dex / 2) including use of the Meditation Skill. Tactical Actions use up a number of Tactical Points equal to 1 + Rank each time they are invoked and Tactical Passives use none.

Ex. Combat Riding I would cost 2 Tactical Points, where as Firearms Mastery IV would use 5.

At Adventurer Creation, an Adventurer can spend 20 Free Skill Points to gain a Rank I Tactical Ability, up to two Rank I abilities in total. No ranks beyond Rank I may be gained in this fashion at Adventurer Creation.

The Cost in Improvement Rolls to gain an ability is equal to its Rank plus 1 but the Adventurer must also fulfill the requirements of the Tactical Ability before taking it. Gaining a Rank I TA requires 2 Improvement Rolls, gaining a rank 2 requires 3 Improvement Rolls and so on. No actual rolls are required to be made, the rolls are simply used up.

Entry Format
Ability Name: The name of the Tactical action. The Roman Numerals following the ability indicate its Rank and in parenthesis, Action or Passive indicate its type.
Requirements: Skill, Trait, or other requirements beyond the Improvement Roll cost to gain the tactical action.
Description: An in-character description of the effect of the tactical action.
Effect: A mechanical description of how the ability works.

Anatomical Precision I (Passive)
Requirements: Medical Training I, First Aid 75%, Combat Style(Small Weapons) 50%

Description: The scalpel has become a constant companion to you. Figuring out where to cut, is second nature and your precision is flawless.

Effect: Your attacks count as one level of success higher for the purposes of getting Combat Manoeuvres when wielding Small size weapons. Your attacks with small weapons also ignore 1 AP.

Combat Riding I (Action)
Requirements: Ride 50%

Description: You have ridden in combat long enough to simply reign your steed with your legs as you make your attacks, allowing you full range of movement with your upper body.

Effect: You can use your full Combat Style score for an attack even if it exceeds your Ride Skill.

Combat Riding II (Action)
Requirements: Ride 75%, Background: Marches or Nomadic

Description: You were practically born in the saddle and know just how to get the most speed out of your mount.

Effect: You can double the speed of your mount with a normal Ride success roll for a single Combat Action. Doing so causes a level of fatigue to your mount but adds an additional step to the Damage Modifier on its attack during that Combat Action.

Cult of Personality I (Passive)
Requirements: 50% Influence OR Courtesy OR Seduction, 12+ CHA

Description: You have cultivated an endearing image of your self using your political wiles. People are more likely to do you a favor because of how well liked you are.

Effect: Add your Influence, Courtesy, or Seduction critical range to the Duty score for political favors. This passive can be taken multiple times to apply to a different organization/skill combination.

Faith I (Passive)
Requirements: Duty 50%, Organization: Any Religion, Rank: Private

Description: Your faith has protected you for as long as you have known.

Effect: For each rank within an organization above Recruit you possess in your religious organization, you have 1 AP that you can place on a single Hit Location. The AP can be moved to other Hit Locations during your daily/weekly prayers or religious ceremonies. Additionally, all Faith effects are disabled for the rest of the day if you fail a persistence roll.

Faith II (Passive)
Requirements: Faith I, Duty 75%, Rank: Sergeant

Description: Your religious awareness has helped you believe in your ability to do anything.

Effect: All of your Organizational Skills from your religion have the critical range of your Duty value added to them and they use the Duty critical range for critical rolls if their critical range is lower. As Faith I, failing a Persistence roll disables this ability for the rest of the day.

Firearms Mastery I (Action)

Requirements: Firearms Combat Style 50%, Mechanisms 50%

Description: You realize there are aiming sights on firearms and have adjusted them enough to aim better at close range.

Effect: You automatically count as having Aimed for 1 CA, regardless of how long you aim, or if you aim at all. (i.e. You aim for 3 CA and add your critical range 4 times to your Combat Style.)

Firearms Mastery II (Action)

Requirements: Firearms Mastery I, Firearms Combat Style 75%

Description: The regular drop of bullets due to gravity has given you an eye for increasing the effective range of your weapon by aiming higher than your sights indicate.

Effect: Attacking beyond the Range value of your weapon only reduces your skill by 25% instead of halving the score. You may attack up to three times the Range Value but attacking beyond double halves your Combat skill. The attacker must aim for at least one Combat Action (not counting the free aim from Rank I).

Firearms Mastery III (Action)

Requirements: Firearms Mastery II, Firearms Combat Style 100%, Organization: Any Military or Technology Organization, Rank: Sergeant

Description: A ready weapon is imperative in times of war, you have loaded your weapon so many times, you have got the process down to mere seconds.

Effect: The Load time of your weapon is halved and by spending an additional Tactical Point, you can make an attack with it in the same CA as the final load. Attacking in this manner does not allow you to move as well.

Firearms Mastery IV (Action)

Requirements: Firearms Mastery III, Mechanisms 100%, Rank: Officer

Description: Multi-shot weapons are a miracle of the modern age and you are an expert in their use, even if it abuses the weapon a little.

Effect: May fire twice the normal rate of fire with a weapon that can fire more than once without loading. Doing so requires a Mechanisms roll with a -20% for each attack made over the normal rate of fire. A failure damages the weapon as if struck by its own attack.

Furious Maul I (Passive)

Requirements: Unarmed or Any 1H (dual wield or single weapon) Combat Style 75%, Brawn 75%

Description: The sight of enemies falling beneath your attacks just propels you to further bloodshed.

Effect: After landing the killing blow to an opponent, you gain one free CA to use immediately, you may only attack as your action but may move normally during the Combat Action.

Hamster Grip I (Passive)

Requirements: Brawn 50%, 2H Axe or Hammer Combat Style 75%, Organization: Cult of Wodin, Rank: Sergeant

Description: Why wield just a single weapon bigger than your entire body? Wodin swung two axes, why shouldn't you?

Effect: You can equip a 2H weapon in one hand, taking a -20% penalty to hit. You may now dual wield 2H Axes or Hammers but only single wield other two-handed weapons.

Just As Planned I (Action)

Requirements: Duty(Any) 75%

Description: You have a preternatural instinct for what to expect, as such you've left missives for your allies, with objectives for them to act out for you.

Effect: Using this ability reduces the time for favors to be enacted down to the minimum time regardless of distance from the source of your favor.

Lead By Example I (Passive)

Requirements: Heroic Command 75%

Description: You've trained extensively with your Squad Mate, so much so you seem to act alike. It may be slight hero worship but your Squad Mate has come to mimic your techniques near exactly.

Effect: Your Squad Mate has the same Tactical Actions you do but they cost an additional Tactical Point to use. Your Squad Mate does not have access to the Tactical Passives.

Medical Training I (Passive)

Requirements: First Aid 50%

Description: You have tested a number of medical drugs and learned which are best for specific issues.

Effect: By making a successful First Aid skill test, you can override the normal priority of Analgesic Powder, purposefully causing a different effect on the patient.

Medical Training II (Action)

Requirements: Medical Training I, First Aid 75%

Description: You refuse to give up on your patients, even in the most dire circumstances you can perform miracles

Effect: Declare the expenditure of a number of Tactical Points, make a successful First Aid roll with a -20% for healing a Serious Injury but no additional penalty for Impalement, Unconsciousness, or Minor Injury. For every Tactical Point spent you perform the normal effect of First Aid and heal an additional 1D2 Hit Points per Tactical Point spent. Using this ability on creatures of a different species will have half the Hit Points restored. This ability cannot heal damage to a Major Injury.

Resuscitation I (Action)

Requirements: Medical Training II, Triage, Healing 75%, Organization: Medical Organization, Rank: Sergeant

Description: Resuscitation techniques are relatively new to medical science but you are one of the early adopters. By a combination of chest compression and assisted breathing techniques, you can bring someone back from the brink of death but the effort drains you emotionally.

Effect: The body of the recently deceased must be present and cannot have any Hit Locations necessary for life detached or dismembered. The medic must begin attempting this ability within 2 Combat Turns of the patient dying. Perform a healing test for each major injury the Adventurer has sustained in their lifetime (at an increasing -10% for each major injury). If all tests are succeeded, a resuscitated Adventurer returns to life with 0 Hit Points on all locations. This Adventurer is still in agony for 2D12 hours and has maximum fatigue. Using this ability expends the rest of the medic's Tactical Points, regardless of how many remain and causes a level of fatigue to the medic. This ability can be used at 0 Tactical Points but the resuscitator suffers an additional level of fatigue from the effort.

Striking Leap I (Action)

Requirements: Fleet Trait or Acrobatics 100%

Description: Powerful leg muscles have allowed you to defy gravity, you can leap into combat with your foes, ignoring what lies between you.

Effect: Can ignore the effects of Terrain and Other Adventurers in your way for one Charge. This Striking Leap Charge can only be performed on foot, not mounted.

Striking Leap II (Action)

Requirements: Striking Leap I, Species: Jumping Mouse, Gerbil, Sardan Pika

Description: You've perfected your aim during a jump, putting your weight and gravity behind your initial attack.

Effect: Increase the Damage Modifier during a Striking Leap Charge by an additional step.

Striking Leap III (Action)

Requirements: Striking Leap II, Organization: Leaping Lancers

Description: Sheer will and bravado have put you with the greatest lancers of the world, your striking leap can clear entire battle lines to hit your target.

Effect: When you have no Fatigue, a Striking Leap Charge has double your movement rate. After the charge is completed, gain a level of fatigue.

Striking Leap IV (Action)

Requirements: Striking Leap III, Rank: Officer

Description: You have learned your lesson to keep moving, *'on the bounce'* and can leap out of combat in the same motion as your striking leap.

Effect: After completing a Striking Leap Charge, the charger can follow through as if mounted but may move in any direction.

Tail Mastery I (Passive)

Requirements: Prehensile Tail Trait

Description: You have used your tail as a third arm long enough to grip weapons steadily and strike with it.

Effect: You may grip weapons in your tail and make attacks with them, gaining an additional Combat Action that can only be used for an attack with your tail weapon. Only Medium or smaller weapons may be held in your tail. Any attacks made with your tail incur a -20% penalty.

Tail Mastery II (Passive)

Requirements: Tail Mastery I, Any Combat Style 50%

Description: You've learned to effectively use your tail in tandem with your normal Combat Style, becoming a whirling storm of death.

Effect: You now incur a reduced penalty of -10% to using your Tail to attack with a weapon. Additionally, you can use your tail to assist in the reloading of weapons, reducing the Load Time by 1 Combat Action.

Tail Mastery III (Passive)

Requirements: Tail Mastery II, Any Combat Style 75%,

Description: Able to curl up your tail and lash out in mere seconds, your opponents rarely expect the extra attack.

Effect: The first attack made with your tail in a combat cannot be parried or evaded.

Tail Mastery IV (Passive)

Requirements: Tail Mastery III, Any two Combat Styles 75%, **Organization**: Assassin's Guild, Rank: Sergeant

Description: Your tail is a vital part of your identity and Combat Style. As an Assassin, you have trained extensively and rely heavily upon it being in good condition.

Effect: Your tail has +2 HP and attacks with it have double the normal critical range for the Combat Style.

Triage I (Action)

Requirements: Medical Training I, Healing 50%

Description: Your Combat Medic training kicks in whenever bullets start flying, you've learned to heal injuries by their priority and get it done quickly.

Effect: First Aid can be performed in 1D3 Combat Actions instead of Minutes. Healing can be performed in 1D3 x10 Combat Actions instead of minutes.

Therapy I (Action)

Requirements: Medical Training I, Influence 50%

Description: In addition to a calming voice, your rapport with patients helps relieve the stress of war.

Effect: By spending 1D2 hours talking to a patient, a Therapist can remove a level of fatigue and increase the patient's Persistence by the Critical range of the Therapist's Influence skill.

Quick Draw I (Action)

Requirements: Firearms 100%, Firearms Mastery II

Description: You've practiced drawing your weapon so many times its second nature to you.

Effect: Drawing a firearm is a free action, you can make an attack with it in the same CA as drawing.

Zealous Strike I (Action)

Requirements: Faith II, Any Melee Combat Style 75%, Organization: Any Religion, Rank: Officer

Description: Your religious fervor empowers you to strike down your foes.

Effect: Add your Duty(Religion) Critical range to your Melee Combat Style and add 1 Damage per rank in the organization when you make an attack.

EQUIPMENT

Melee Weapons

Weapon	Damage	STR/DEX	Size	Reach	Combat Maneuvers	ENC	AP/HP	Cost
1H Firearm Butt	1D2	-/-	S	S	Stun Location	-	-	-
2H Firearm Butt	1D4	-/-	M	M	Stun Location	-	-	-
Axe Bayonet	2D4	10/9	M	M	Bleed, Sunder	1	3/6	5 GM
Bayonet	1D6	8/9	S	L	Impale	-	4/6	1 GM
Claw Gauntlet	1D6+1	12/-	M	S	Bleed, Impale	1	6/6	10 GM
Entrenching Shovel	1D6	5/-	M	S	Bleed	1	4/4	1 GM
Tail Blade	1D4+1	7/12	S	S	Bleed	-	4/6	5 GM

Axe Bayonet

A small axe head that is attached to the bottom of a rifle. Although this provides a more formidable melee weapon over a regular bayonet, the extra weight disrupts your shooting ability even more. Attaching an Axe Bayonet to a 2H Firearm allows you to attack with it in melee instead of 2H Firearm Butt but applies a -20% to hit with a normal firearm ranged attack.

Bayonet

A small knife or blade that is attached to the bottom of a rifle. This provides a better reach and penetrating power than simply hitting your melee opponent with the rifle butt. Attaching a bayonet to a 2H Firearm allows you to attack with it in melee instead of 2H firearm butt but applies a -10% to hit with a normal firearm ranged attack.

Claw Gauntlet - One Handed

A metal gauntlet with razor-like claws that fit over the Adventurer's own claws. Uses the Unarmed skill as its Combat Style.

Entrenching Shovel - One Handed

A shovel that is serrated to help it cut through tough dirt, roots and even soft stone. Attacking with an Entrenching Shovel ignores 1 point of armor. Outside of combat an Entrenching Shovel gives +10% to Brawn when digging.

Tail Blade

A weapon that can be strapped to a Large Tail to provide an additional attack as if the Adventurer had Prehensile Tail and Tail Mastery I. Such attacks use the Unarmed Skill and have a -20% penalty.

2H/1H Firearm butt

This is not a real weapon but the profile for using a 2H or 1H firearm as a club. Pistols may be used in close combat with their normal profile but to continue attacking after you have run out of loaded shots, this is used instead. The Combat Style is represented by Brawn.

Range Weapons

Weapon	Damage	Dam Mod	Range	Load	STR/ DEX	Skill	ENC	AP/ HP	Cost
30 Pound Cannon	1D12	No	200m	6	10/12	Artillery	X	5/10	500 GM
Ballista	1D8	No	100m	4	10/12	Artillery	X	4/10	300 GM
Efrit Cannon	1D12	No	200m	6/4	12/12	Artillery	X	5/10	500 GM
Hand Mortar	X	No	35m	4	9/9	Firearms	3	4/7	35 GM
Heavy Pistol	2D6	No	50m	3/1	6/9	Firearms	1	4/4	15 GM
Light Rifle	2D6	No	75m	3/1	7/11	Firearms	2	4/7	25 GM
Light Panzardi	2D6	No	25m	3/20	12/14	Firearms	4	4/10	250 GM
Long Rifle	2D8	No	100m	4/1	8/11	Firearms	3	4/8	50 GM
Naptha Bomb (5)	2D8	No	3m	--	7/9	Throwing	1	4/3	5 GM
Panzardi Speciale	2D6	No	50m	2/20	10/12	Artillery	5*	4/10	200 GM
Pocket Pistol	2D4	No	25m	2/1	5/9	Firearms	1	4/3	10 GM
Repeater	1D8	No	50m	3/3	8/10	Firearms	2	4/8	50 GM
Shrapnel Grenade (5)	4D6	No	3m	--	11/9	Throwing	1	4/3	5 GM
Sapper's Dynamite	4D10	No	5m	--	-/-	--	2	2/3	15 GM
Shotgun	4D4*	No	30m	3/2	9/9	Firearms	3	4/7	35 GM
Venturan Mortar	X	No	50m	2	10/12	Artillery	5*	4/10	250 GM
York Pistol	1D6	No	25m	3/4	6/9	Firearms	1	4/4	15 GM

Firearms & Artillery

Any weapon that is classified as a firearm or Artillery does not use 2xDEX to derive its Combat Style. These weapons use DEX+INT to determine starting skill. Any Adventurer can shoot a firearm as if they had the firearm Combat Style at its basic value but must reload the weapon as if it had a 2x load time. Taking the Combat Style returns the load time to its normal value.

Pistols are offhanded weapons and can be used in a two weapon style with small-size ranged weapons or one handed melee weapons. Loading a pistol still requires two hands free. Pistols also cannot be parried or evaded in close combat.

Rifles bullets move so fast and hit so hard that most armor is useless in an age of gunpowder. Rifles ignore half armor on a Hit Location. This does not affect natural armor, only equipped armor.

Firearms have different shot capacities, as such, Load will indicate both the load time and the attack count before having to reload in this format X/Y, X being Load, Y being attack count.

Deviation - When throwing or shooting grenades and other explosives, should the attack fail to hit the target but not cause a fumble, the explosive will deviate 2 meters per 10% you miss by. Roll 1D8 to determine direction. (1 Being North, 2 North East, etc.)

Explosive Range - The Range listed for Shrapnel Grenades, Naphtha Bombs, Sapper's Dynamite and other explosives indicates the Area of Effect rather than the range of the attack. The throwing range is based off the Athletics skill as detailed in the *Legend Core Rulebook*.

30 Pound Cannon - Two Handed, Three Operators

This cannon has wheeled mounting if used in the field, or a rolling block if mounted to a ship or castle wall. Cannons are innately inaccurate and firing one requires a -20% penalty to Combat Style (Artillery). Regardless of ammunition used, the cannon deals its damage to targets hit by its attack, in addition to any other effects. The Cannon is too heavy to be carried by Adventurers. It can be pulled using Brawn, 5 meters per 10% Brawn per minute. The cannon may also be drawn by a steed at half movement rate after taking a minute to harness the cannon to the steed.

Ballista - Two Handed, Two Operators

A large crossbow mounted to the back of a Siege Tortoise or built with a frame to stabilize it on the ground. If fired from the back of a tortoise while moving it suffers -20% to Combat Style (Artillery). The ballista fires large crossbow bolts that pass through unarmored targets but always impale armored targets. If a bolt passes through an unarmored target it can hit one additional target before losing momentum. The damage ignores armor. The ballista is too heavy to be carried by Adventurers. It can be pushed using Brawn, 2 meters per 10% Brawn per minute.

Efrit Cannon - Two Handed, Two Operators

This Rapid-fire Cannon comes with mounting to strap it to a Siege Tortoise, allowing it to move and fire. The drawback of this style of artillery is that Combat Style (Artillery) is halved if the tortoise has moved during the turn the weapon is fired, otherwise it suffers a -20% for the basic inaccuracy of cannons. Two operators must be riding the tortoise to load and fire its weapon. Regardless of which ammunition is used in the cannon, it deals its damage to targets hit by its attack, in addition to any other effects. The Cannon is too heavy to be carried by Adventurers. It can be pushed using Brawn, 1 meter per 10% Brawn per minute.

Hand Mortar - Two Handed

A two handed, large tube that operates similar to a regular firearm but is large enough to use Shrapnel Grenades, or Naphtha Bombs as ammunition. Firing a grenade or bomb in this fashion increases the range to 35m and uses the Firearms Skill instead of Throwing. Hand Mortars are notoriously dangerous weapons, the critical failure range is 95-100. A critical failure means the bomb has not left the mortar and the fuse is still ticking down. A successful engineering roll at -20% lets you attempt to fire again on the next Combat Action. If the fuse runs out, it destroys the Hand Mortar and applies its damage as normal where you tossed the hand mortar as you ran for it.

Heavy Pistol - One Handed

An older, larger breech loading pistol, classically used in duels. Their increased size allows a larger caliber ammunition than a Pocket Pistol.

Light Panzardi - Two Handed

The one-man handheld version of the Panzardi Speciale, is an absurd weapon. For safety reasons it fires at a slower rater than the Speciale, making 3 attacks at a -30% penalty in a single Combat Action. The sweeping rate is much easier, able to turn 90 degrees in a single Combat Action. Like a Speciale the Light Panzardi can continue firing over multiple Combat Actions and incurs a -10% penalty to mechanism rolls to make sure the gun does not jam or overheat. Unlike the Speciale, the Light Panzardi has no mounting but a user that moves over half their movement rate suffers an additional -10% to hit on any attacks after moving.

Light Rifle - Two Handed

Breach loaded light rifles are the standard issue weapon in most armies, as their loading is much simpler than a Long rifle and they are cheaper to produce and supply ammunition for than Repeater Carbines. Their ammunition sits in between Carbines and Long Rifles in caliber and gunpowder charge providing a decent mid-range weapon.

Long Rifle - Two Handed

Older Muzzle-loaded rifles are still the preferred weapon of snipers as their increased range compared to cased ammunition rifles is key to counter-balancing their long load times.

Naphtha Bomb - One Handed, Explosive

A conflagration explosive, that deals its damage by setting its victims on fire. When you throw the bomb, the GM secretly rolls 1D6, this determines how many Combat Actions pass before the bomb detonates. If time remains, someone can pick up the grenade and chuck it back, or dive for cover. Either way, when the bomb detonates it deals its total damage to each target, ignoring 1/2 their armor and applies Large Flame damage. This Fire damage continues each turn until the fire is put out via water, suffocation or other means. The base damage from the bomb is split amongst 2D4 Hit Locations but the Large Flame damage applies in total to each Hit Location. The GM should also be sure to note that the Naphtha bomb will apply its damage to everything else in range, including inanimate objects. If any of the dice rolled for damage are a result of '1' that die's value is ignored; if all dice are '1's the bomb is a dud. Naphtha Bombs are one use weapons.

Panzardi Speciale - Two Handed, Two Operators
A unique weapon design from the city of Venture, the Speciale is a two-man operated, automatic loading, self-powered machine gun. In a single Combat Action, the Speciale fires 5 Times at a -20% penalty, counting as 5 shots out of 20 from its total load. Each attack can be made at targets in a sweeping arc in front of the machine gun. At maximum range, the Speciale can sweep over the course of its 5 attacks 15 meters. Each time the Panzardi Speciale continues firing without pausing for at least a Combat Action, the operators must make a mechanisms roll at an increasing -10% penalty to keep it operating smoothly. If the roll is failed, the Gun jams and is damaged equal to the damage of the attack. The barrel must be cleared and the firing mechanisms repaired before operation can continue. For every Turn that the gun is not in use without having been damaged, the mechanisms penalty is reduced by 10%. When not in operation, the Panzardi Speciale is broken down into two major components, the gun itself and its mounting. Breaking down for movement takes One Combat Action from each operator and each Operator takes 5 ENC to carry their half of the machine. Setting up in another position takes another Combat Action from each operator. Safety mechanisms keep the gun from firing without resting on its mounting.

Pocket Pistol - One Handed
Easily concealable but low caliber, the Pocket pistol is a defensive weapon, best at extremely close ranges. They are breach loading weapons and only about the size of your paw, lending their other nickname as 'paw pistols'.

Repeater Carbine - Two Handed
Smaller build rifles that are capable of loading more than one round at a time and fire them in succession before needing to reload. Repeater Carbines are coming into their own as a law enforcement and cavalry weapon, allowing single shooters to hold off multiple assailants. To keep the weight down smaller ammunition is used, reducing the overall damage and range.

Sapper's Dynamite - Two Handed, Explosive

Mining and Wrecking explosives, Dynamite is detonated by a plunger and cord, or by a sudden shock to the nitroglycerin laced through it. Packs of dynamite are too heavy to throw any real distance and use in warfare is usually reserved for laying traps, or sapping structures. The range of sapper's dynamite is based on the total length of detonation cord. A regular purchase of Sapper's Dynamite includes 20m of cord. Proper use entails placing the dynamite where you wish it to detonate and then running the cord back to the plunger and depressing the plunger to detonate it. Dynamite is a one use weapon, the cord and plunger can be reused, giving a 2 GM discount on new dynamite charges.

Shrapnel Grenade - One Handed, Explosive

A gunpowder explosive that is loaded with pieces of metal, designed to deal damage more from the debris than from the explosive charge. When you throw the grenade, the GM secretly rolls 1D6 , this determines how many Combat Actions pass before the grenade detonates. If time remains, someone can pick up the grenade and chuck it back, or dive for cover. Either way, when the grenade detonates it deals its total damage to each target. On targets with Hit Locations, the damage is split amongst 2D4 Hit Locations, ignoring half armor before applying to health. If any of the dice rolled for damage are a result of '1' that die's value is ignored; if all dice are '1's the bomb is a dud. Grenades are one use weapons.

Shotgun - Two Handed

Also known as a trenchgun for its perfect scene of use, the Shotgun shoots a pack of small pellets at the target. As the energy and focus of the pellets is lost over a distance but is perfect at close ranges, the damage from 15m or closer adds +4 to the total rolled. Beyond 30m the damage is reduced to 3D4. Shotguns ignore one point of armor, rather than half like rifles but can be equipped with bayonets.

Venturan Mortar - Two Handed, Two Operators

Built on the same mounting as the Panzardi Speciale, the Venturan Mortar is a stabilized version of the Hand Mortar. Like a hand mortar, the Venturan Mortar can be loaded with Shrapnel Grenades or Naphtha Bombs, firing in the same manner. The mortar cannot be moved while firing and must be broken down like a Panzardi Speciale.

York Pistol - One Handed

A multi-barreled pistol, popular with naval officers, privateers and cavalry soldiers as a side arm. The multiple barrels can be loaded and fired individually, or by a trick of the triggering mechanisms, can be all fired instantly, adding the damage from each loaded round to the attack (dealing 4D6 with 4 bullets loaded). Firing all the barrels at once requires your other hand free to reduce the shock or suffer 1 damage to the arm holding the weapon (ignoring armor).

Ammunition

Ammunition	ENC	Cost
18mm Muzzle with Paper Cartridges (10)	-	5 SM
.22 Short Cased (20)	-	5 SM
.44 Long Cased (10)	-	3 SM
00 Rat-Shot (10)	1	5 SM
12 Gauge Snake-Slug (5)	1	5 SM
Ballista Bolt (2)	2	5 SM
Efrit Round Shot	3	10 SM
Efrit Shrapnel Shell	3	12 SM
Large Round Shot	4	12 SM
Large Chain Shot	4	12 SM
Panzardi Ring Magazine (20)	1	15 SM

18mm Muzzle with Paper Cartridges - Long Rifle Ammo

Conical shaped bullets that are the last hold outs for muzzle loaded ammunition, 18mm Muzzle rounds are used by Long Rifles. The enormous size of these rounds is known to cause actual dismemberment of limbs. Luckily for the targets, the loading of these shots still requires a ramrod and separate powder cartridges, slowing the rate of fire immensely.

.22 Short Cased - Repeater Carbine and Pocket Pistol Ammo

One of the early shell cased bullet designs, the .22 Short is loaded into Repeater Carbines and Pocket Pistols. The shorter case reduces the total gunpowder in the shell, reducing the force and range but keeps the user unencumbered when dealing with a lot more ammunition than other weapons.

.44 Long Cased - Light Rifle and Heavy Pistol Ammo

A more recent design for breech loading Light Rifles and Heavy Pistols, these larger bullets with a larger powder load hit hard and have a decent range to them. These bullets are unfortunately a little more expensive due to the resources involved.

.44 Short Cased - York Pistol Ammo

Originally the first York pistols used .44 Longs but the force of firing all the rounds at once broke the wrists of users, so a smaller Short case was designed, this unfortunately reduced the overall damage and range but allowed the user to keep their arm out of a sling.

00 Rat-Shot - Shotgun Ammo

Pronounced 'Double Aught', the Rat-shot is a shotgun shell with about eight lead pellets packed in front of a large gunpowder charge. It was so named for its ability to take down rats who had succumbed to disease during the Ermindorf Riots.

12 Gauge Snake-Slug - Shotgun Ammo

Designed by the Aquitaran Foreign Legion for use against larger creatures, these solid slugs are an alternative ammunition for a shotgun. Using these more expensive shells makes the bonus adds 1D4 to the total damage and makes it ignore half armor like a rifle.

Ballista Bolt - Ballista Ammo

A large crossbow bolt, with more in common with a spear or javelin. The ballista bolt has high penetrating power and has been the go-to siege weapon of civilizations without gunpowder for centuries. The lower price of such weapons even makes them common for smaller armies in modern times.

Efrit Solid Shot - Efrit Cannon Ammo

A cased cannon ball sized to fit the bore of an Efrit Cannon. The force of the cannon ball impacts a target hard enough to instantly cause a Serious Injury to a Hit Location or a Major Injury on a failed Resilience test. The victim and anyone else within 5 meters suffer the cannon's damage spread across 2D4 Hit Locations, ignoring armor. This attack deviates on a failure.

Efrit Shrapnel Shell - Efrit Cannon Ammo

A hollow shell filled with metal bearings that burst from the shell about 10 meters out of the cannon. The bearings then spread out hitting a number of targets. Starting 10 meters out from the Cannon, this attack affects a 15m wide, 20m long area. The cannon's damage is multiplied by 1D6 then spread across 2D4 Hit Locations (roll independently for each victim). These attacks do not ignore armor and shrapnel is too small to damage sturdy structures. This attack is very hard to dodge. Shrapnel shell does not suffer from -20% inaccuracy but instead, for every 10% by which you miss, targets suffer 1 less multiplier on the 1D6. (A Shell misses by 20% and the attack rolled a 5 multiplier. The attacker rolls 3D12 for damage to the target.)

Large Chain Shot - 30 Pound Cannon Ammo

A hollow cannon ball cut in half with a chain linking the halves. The chain shot is designed to spin after being fired from a cannon, creating a wide cutting path, usually for breaking the masts of ships. Chain shot will easily go through wood walls without stopping. If a target is struck by a chain shot, it instantly suffers a Major Injury to a

Hit Location and it is severed from the body. The Chain shot continues moving past its first victim but the spinning effect is lost and it only does the cannon's damage to one Hit Location of its next target before losing too much momentum to be a continued threat. This damage does not ignore armor. This attack deviates on a failure.

Large Round Shot - 30 Pound Cannon Ammo
A larger cannon ball sized to fit the 30 Pounder. The force of the cannon ball impacts a target hard enough to instantly cause a Serious Injury to a Hit Location or a Major Injury on a failed Resilience test. Anyone within 5 meters suffer a serious Injury to a Hit Location on a failed Resilience test. The victim and anyone else within 5 meters suffer the cannon's damage spread across 2D4 Hit Locations, ignoring armor. This attack deviates on a failure.

Panzardi Ring Magazine - Panzardi Speciale and Light Panzardi Ammo
The Ring shaped magazine used by the Panzardi Speciale and its smaller counterpart contains 20 8mm Long-Cased rounds that are spring fed by the magazine into the Speciale. The hole in the center of the Ring makes it easy for the second operator to carry multiple magazines, or hang them from the mounting of the gun while reloading, letting the gunner continue firing.

Armor

Type	AP	ENC	Cost Per Hit Location
Cotton	1	0	10 SM
Hard Leather	2	2	15 SM
Linen	2	1	20 SM
Ringmail	3	2	40 SM
Scalemail	4	2	50 SM
Chain Mail	5	3	80 SM
Plate	6	3	150 SM
Articulated Plate	7	4	300 SM

Effects of SIZ on Armor
Unlike in *Legend*, SIZ has no bearing on the ENC of armor. Half the cost for Tiny species and Double the price for every other size bracket beyond Large.

Cotton
The most common form of protection, be it a heavy coat or thick clothing, everyone is used to wearing this fabric. As such, no Armor Penalty is applied to your Strike Rank when wearing cotton armor.

Items

Item	ENC	Cost
Analgesic Powder	1	5 SM
Assault Assistance Pack	5	200 GM
AAP Charge (1)	1	10 GM
Carbolic Soap	1	2 SM
Detonation Cord	-	5 SM
Healer's Kit	1	50 SM
Magnesia Compound (5)	1	5 SM
Valkyr Mk.1 Clockwork Armor	-	500 GM

Analgesic Powder

Painkillers have existed since ancient times but the modern powders created by pharmacists prove to be generally safer for regular use. Doses of Analgesic Powder can provide a number of effects but they are not miracle drugs, they will always apply to the first effect in the order listed that the user has.

1. Remove a level of fatigue for 12 hours.
2. Ignore the non-damaging effects of a poison or disease for 12 hours.
3. Ignore the effects of a failed Resilience roll for a serious wound for 6 hours.
4. A sufferer from a major wound doubles the time before they die from the wound.
5. Heals 2 HP to all locations but suffer a -10% to all physical Skill Tests for 12 hours.

After applying an Analgesic, additional doses within 12 hours provide no beneficial effect and can actually be detrimental, causing a stacking -10% to all rolls for each overdose. Beyond 4 doses, levels of fatigue are applied for doses.

Assault Assistance Pack

An invention of the Skyguard, the AAP is a short burst rocket that 'assists' the user in jumping gaps, say from the deck of an airship to a castle parapet. The AAP works slightly different from a normal jump under the Athletics skill:

Mechanism rolls determines if the AAP was used properly, a failure means the device failed to start, a critical failure means the device will detonate in 1D6 Combat Actions as a Naphtha Bomb. A Critical Success lets you pick the exact spot you land between 21-30 meters.

A running jump with an AAP provides no benefit compared to a standing jump.

The AAP makes a jump of 1D10+20 meters horizontally, with a required vertical clearance of 1D6+10 meters.

You take fall damage one damage category lower than normal if the landing position is below your launch position; the AAP cushions your landing slightly.

Every point of SIZ above 10 reduces the distance by ½ meter

Every point of Armor Penalty reduces the distance by ½ meter

Four Charges are installed into an AAP at a time, allowing 4 jumps before requiring new charges need to be loaded.

Replacing 4 Charges requires one mechanisms roll, failure to install the charges properly damages a charge, wasting it and requires another mechanism roll to install the remaining charges. Critical Success allows you to avoid Mechanism rolls for the use of the AAP until the next installation. Critical Failure results in damage to all the charges and you need to purchase a new set.

Carbolic Soap

Cleanliness in surgery and other medical procedures is a recent development, before the papers published by David Lister on the topic of antiseptics and germ theory, 'miasma' was the supposed cause of disease. Carbolic Soap is now the standard tool for germ killing and sterilization of a surgery room. Use of soap provides a +10% bonus to First Aid and Healing Skill Tests. To get the proper effect, an entire bar is used up in performing Healing rolls but only half a bar for First Aid.

Detonation Cord

To put a larger distance between you and your dynamite, additional detonation cord adds 5m per section purchased to the total distance you can be from the dynamite and still detonate it.

Healer's Kit

See *Legend Core Rulebook*. Works the same, only a price change is made to this item.

Magnesia Compound

A chemically prepared vial of Magnesium Hydroxide, when mixed with water creates a make-shift antivenom by encouraging the digestive system. When ingested, provides a 1D10+10 bonus to the imbiber's Resilience Score. The Magnesia Compound results in a laxative effect and the imbiber will need to resolve their digestive issues after resisting the venom.

Valkyr Mk. I Clockwork Armor

The premier tool of the Valkyr Corp. and invention of Federwerk Industries, the Valkyr is a clockwork suit of armor, that augments the combat abilities of its user. Designed for an intelligent operator, the Engineering and Mechanisms skill critical range of the operator are added to various skills while used in a Valkyr. Basic Valkyr have the statistics listed in the Mounts & Beasts of Burden Section. They can equip any weapons that an Adventurer can but weapons must be integrated into a Valkyr by spending 1d3 hours converting the weapon, mounting it to an arm and making a Mechanisms roll. A failure renders the weapon useless, a critical failure renders the mounting arm useless, both requiring repair to make them useful again. Uninstalling a weapon follows the same basic rules as installing a weapon. You must be Tiny or Small size category to pilot a Valkyr.

Mounts & Beasts of Burden

Disregard this section of the *Legend Core Rulebook*, the following Mounts and Beasts of Burden are available in the Eutheria region of Brushfire.

Mount	ENC Carried	Cost
Plough Kiwi	70	200 GM
Riding Kiwi	50	250 GM
Riding Turtle	75	300 GM
Siege Tortoise	250	1000 GM

Kiwi - Avian Steed

	Dice	Average	
STR	2D6+18	25	
CON	3D6+6	17	
SIZ	1D6+13	17	Large
INT	4	4	
DEX	3D6+3	10	
CHA	2+1D10	8	

1D20	Hit Location	AP/HP
1–5	Right Leg	2/7
6–10	Left Leg	2/7
11–16	Body	2/17
17–20	Head	2/7

Combat Actions	2
Damage Modifier	+1D8
Movement	16m
Strike Rank	+7

Typical Armor: Hide (2 AP) , No Armor penalty
Traits: Medium Mount
Skills: Athletics 75%, Brawn 60%, Persistence 45%, Resilience 60%, Survival 20%

Combat Styles
Kick 40%, Peck 60%

Weapons

Type	Size	Reach	Damage	AP/HP
Kick	M	M	1D6+1D8	As for Leg
Peck	M	L	2D6+1D8	As for Leg

Medium Mount

Kiwis are large enough to carry Medium or smaller creatures as riders.

Creature Notes

   A strange, flightless bird, that came to Eutheria along trade routes from the southeast. They instantly became popular as domesticated steeds and are heavily used in the marchlands between Aquitar and Vandalands. Two basic varieties of Kiwi exist. The Plough Kiwi is used by farmers to till their fields and perform other civilian tasks such as pulling carts or carriages, These Kiwis have a higher ENC value as noted in the Equipment section but they suffer a -20% to all skills if forced into combat including applying a -20% to the Ride skill of the rider. Riding Kiwis are trained for battle or scouting and have no issues carrying soldiers into battle.

Riding Turtle - Reptilian Steed

	Dice	Average		1D20	Hit Location	AP/HP
STR	2D6+18	25		1–3	Right Rear Leg	4/8
CON	4D6+10	17		4–6	Left Rear Leg	4/8
SIZ	1D6+16	20	Very Large	7-9	Right Fore Leg	4/8
INT	4	4		10-12	Left Fore Leg	4/8
DEX	1D6+3	7		13–18	Body	6/19
CHA	2D6+4	11		19–20	Head	4/8

Combat Actions	2
Damage Modifier	+1D8
Movement	6m
Strike Rank	+7

Typical Armor: Turtle Shell (3 AP) , No Armor penalty
Traits: Large Mount
Skills: Athletics 60%, Brawn 80%, Persistence 70%, Resilience 80%, Survival 20%

Combat Styles
Snap 60%

Weapons

Type	Size	Reach	Damage	AP/HP
Snap	M	M	2D6+1D8	As for Head

Large Mount
Riding Turtles are large enough to carry Large Size or smaller riders.

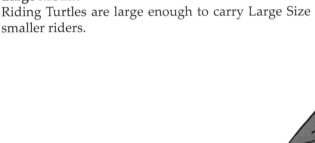

Creature Notes

Unlike their northern relatives, the Turtles of Bharat are non-sapient and have been domesticated by the Geckos for centuries. After the collapse of the Bharatese nations, the Geckos fled across the sea to Scyzantium and their riding turtles came with them. These lumbering mounts provide a rather stable platform for shooting from, allowing a rider's Combat Style to exceed their Ride skill by 15%. Special mountings on Riding Turtles are designed for the use of Long Rifles, allowing Combat Style to exceed Ride by 25% when firing one.

Siege Tortoise - Reptilian Steed

	Dice	Average		1D20	Hit Location	AP/HP
STR	2D6+20	27		1–3	Right Leg	4/10
CON	2D6+20	27		4–6	Left Leg	4/10
SIZ	1D6+25	29	Giant	7-9	Right Fore Leg	4/10
INT	2D6+8*	15		10-12	Left Fore Leg	4/10
DEX	1D6+3	7		13–18	Body	8/23
CHA	2+1D10	8		19–20	Head	4/10

*+1D6 for every 100 years of age past the first.

Combat Actions	2
Damage Modifier	+1D12
Movement	12m
Strike Rank	+7

Typical Armor: Hide (4 AP), Turtle Shell (8 AP), No Armor penalty
Traits: Huge Mount
Skills: Athletics 75%, Brawn 60%, Persistence 45%, Resilience 60%, Survival 20%

Combat Styles
Snap 60%

Weapons

Type	Size	Reach	Damage	AP/HP
Snap	M	L	2D6+1D12	As for Head

Huge Mount

Siege Tortoises are able to carry a Huge or smaller creature, or carry a Howdah and up to 3 Large or smaller creatures. Artillery may also be mounted to the Siege Tortoise.

Creature Notes

Indigenous to the Island of Adwaita and the surrounding mainland, the Siege Tortoises form symbiotic relationships with the Anoles that are also indigenous to Adwaita. These massive creature are able to be used as walking siege weapons, either as rams, smashing their weight into castle walls, or by strapping cannons or other massive weapons to their shells. When travelling, Howdahs are often strapped to them so that several riders can travel in style. The extreme lifespan of the Siege Tortoises allow them to share their knowledge with their Anole companions, often being paired several times over their life, as the Anoles lifespan is much shorter than their own.

Valkyr Mk. 1 - Clockwork Armor

	Dice	Average		1D20	Hit Location	AP/HP
STR	2D6+18	25		1–3	Right Leg	4/4
SIZ	1D6+13	17	Large	4–6	Left Leg	4/4
DEX	3D6+3	10		7-12	Body	8/11
				13-15	Right Arm	4/3
Damage Modifier		+1D8		16-18	Left Arm	4/3
Movement		6m/10m		19–20	Engine	4/4

Typical Armor: Iron Skin (4 AP) / Hardy Wood (3 AP), No Armor Penalty
Traits: Small Pilot, Mechanical, Gyro-stable, Buoyant OR Water Tight
Skills: Athletics 50%, Evade 25%, Brawn 75%, Resilience 75%, Survival 20%

Combat Styles
Unarmed or Any Combat Style 65%

Weapons
May Equip Two Weapons, ignoring STR/DEX restrictions and One/Two-handedness

Small Pilot
 Valkyr are large enough to carry Small or Tiny creatures as pilots. Pilots are contained within a Valkyr and replace their physical skills with those of the Valkyr. These skills are augmented by adding the Engineering and Mechanisms critical range of the pilot to their scores as follows:

Engineering
 Melee Combat Styles
 Unarmed
 Brawn
 Stealth

Mechanisms
 Ranged Combat Styles
 Athletics
 Resilience
 Sleight

Highest of the Two
Evade

Mechanical
 Cannot be affected by biological agents such as Poison or Disease. These can affect the pilot if the attack that applied poison or disease hit the Body and did enough damage to exceed the AP value of the Body. The Valkr's Combat Actions and Strike Rank are determined by the Pilot. If the Body or Engine of a Valkyr reaches 0, suffering a serious 'injury' and a Resilience test is failed, the Valkyr will explode as a Shrapnel Grenade in 1D6 Combat Actions. The pilot takes 2 Combat Actions to escape the vehicle. Upon suffering a major 'injury' to the Body or Engine the Valkyr will explode as a Shrapnel Grenade in 1D3 Combat Actions, a successful Resilience test adds +1 Combat Action to the time on the grenade, giving the pilot precious seconds to escape.

Gyro-Stable

The only reason these machines can stay upright is the gyroscopes that keep them balanced. These spinning metal disks use angular momentum to stabilize every action including sharp movement. When Evading, make a Mechanisms or Engineering roll with a -20% penalty. On a success, the Valkyr does not fall prone in a successful evade and can act normally.

Buoyant OR Water Tight

Valkyr are alternatively made of Porous yet hardy woods found around Federwerk, or of a Steel alloy mined in the mountains. Each provides a different effect. Buoyant Wood material Makes the Valkyr float in water, automatically succeeding swim checks but the Armor value of the Valkyr is reduced by 1 on all Hit Locations. Water Tight Metal Valkyr sink straight to the bottom of water but are able to walk normally across the bottom, unfortunately they do not include extra air beyond 1D4 minutes.

Creature Notes

A clockwork, robotic armor built to allow smaller creatures to become soldiers and effectively combat the larger creatures of the world. Piloting a Valkyr requires a Mechanisms or Engineering Skill of at least 40% to pilot. These come in a variety of formats but the Mk. 1 is the most basic and common version.

Map of Eutheria
1825 AF

HISTORY OF THE WORLD

The Titanic Age

Before the recorded age of mammals and reptiles, a race of insects ruled every continent. Only the mountains, through which they could not dig, remained free of their influence. These creatures are known by a dozen names; The Titans, to the Hyperians, Obakemono to the Ribenguans, Khepri to the Khonshans and Daemons to the Rodentians. In modern times they are known as exomorphs, for their unique exoskeletal biology. These creatures had no language of their own, barely able to mimic the sounds of 'endomorphs', those with internal skeletons. As each exomorph knew what his hive-kin knew, no history, culture, or art is recorded from this time. The few artifacts that remain were treated as cursed relics, symbols of demons and monsters. The first recorded is quoted at the beginning of the Rodeniad, 'On the day the sky burned bright, when the heroes rose against their rulers and slew them, the lesser titans disappeared below the earth'. Since the end of the Titanic age, they have resurfaced many times.

Excerpt from The Rodeniad

They thought that Alexandreta was secure. An island more than a mile off the coast, multiple walls of protection and enough farmland to support an army. Now the alliance was collapsing. The birds flew from their roosts leaving the mammals and reptiles to die. The Titans had come from everywhere at once. Bursting from below the earth, every nation was overrun. While the mountainous regions were immune to the creatures, leaving much of the north and the east free, the small tribes that lived there were of no use to them now. Pacing the halls, trailed by his advisers, Tydeus, the Tyrant of Hyperia, will have no more words with his counterpart. Pharaoh Menemer, young on his throne, prays to the moon, symbol of Khonshu, for guidance.

Menemer retraces his lineage to Wadjet, the snake king that had overthrown the Khepri. The Khepri or Titans now amassed beyond the inner wall of the island city. As Menemer prayed for victory over these monsters, his bodyguard, Tiamat, came to his side. Tiamat, High Guard of the Pharaoh, was scarred from many battles against the Khepri. Her blade had been notched many times against the carapace of the enemy. In a recent battle she had protected her lord against the insidious Pazuzu, Khepri of the sky. As they had retreated to Alexandreta, she had been wounded by the poisonous sting of the flying monsters. Many of their ships had returned to dock with barely a soul alive. Tiamat did not have time to die.

Rodenalus, inventor and last true citizen of Alexandreta, tinkered in his workshop. His assistants had fled when the armies first came to convert the city of science into a city of war. He had remained however, intent upon continuing his work. He stopped his work and listened to the scratching in the walls. The Titans were just beyond that wall digging through the soft dirt but unable to break the solid of the fortress. It was beyond their greatest imagining that the Titants that did not fly like the harpies could in order to reach the island city. This illusion was shattered as they tunnelled beneath the sea floor, past fissures and floods, to erupt into the outer courtyard, where the farms had supplied the united armies for months and the scientists before that. The young inventor was sure that they were hunting for his creation. For what other reason would these mindless monsters seek out this isolated citadel? He was resigned however, both to his death and to never seeing his creation fight on the battlefield. From outside he heard commotion. The flapping of wings, a crash and cries for help from the soldiers in the inner keep.

The left wing of Tengri would no longer hold him aloft, between his wound and his armor, he quickly came to the earth. As he screeched in pain from the arrow in his wing, guards rushed toward him. In their panic at a shadow across the sun, several Hyperian soldiers had attacked the bird. Care was given immediately and the generals and kings gathered around the messenger. Tengri had come with word of the Erlik movements on the mainland. As a scout, he was unaware of the withdrawal of his people from the alliance. In a few days he was well enough to share his knowledge.

Far to the east, beyond the bird city of Mawenzi, beyond the jungles of Zabar, in the ocean of Bharat, lay Lemuria, a Bahamutian, a sea creature larger than an island. It was on its back that the hive laid its eggs. Digging deep within the whale, the Erlik had seized control of it. It was slowly moving toward Alexandreta. It was a few weeks away but its mass would crush the walls and send forth thousands of monsters upon the defenders. If it was not stopped before reaching the shores of the fortress, a second Titanic age would come and all civilizations would fall. Despite his hyperbole, Tengri's message was heard by Tydeus and Menmer. Each ruler set a plan before the war council. They fought for days over the one that would be followed. As their differences placed a wedge between them, no compromise could be met.

Tiamat spent her days speaking with Tengri, the two discussed the situation and alternatives that could be sought. On one of their walks through the fortress, they came upon Rodenalus in his workshop, completing the last adjustments to his Manticore. With the completed weapon before them, the three hatched a plan to win the minds of the Tyrant and the Pharaoh.

Rodenalus had long had the ear of Tydeus, it was their friendship that allowed him to continue his work at the fortress. He displayed the operation of his machine for the Tyrant, moving the device into the courtyard. It was the first time the machine had seen the light of day since its carapace had been slain by Tydeus' myrmidons. The massive pincers crushed the shield and armor of a target dummy and its tail fired bolts into Harpies as they flew over the keep. Both operations acted in unison and worked perfectly. Tydeus was impressed but not moved to lay his plans aside for Rodenalus' machine. Rodenalus spoke to Tydeus of Menmer's hate of the machine and Hyperian science. With that simplest mention, Tydeus lept upon the new plan and agreed to it instantly, intent upon showing the Khonshan king the superiority of Hyperian inventions. Tiamat did not have to lie to Menmer, the young king followed her every advice and when she pressed the plan to him, Menmer acquiesced. With the alliance agreed, their plan was set in motion.

The Manticore broke down the inner gates, sending chunks of wood and iron out into the trampled farmlands. Its operators hidden within its chitinous carapace remained uninjured as the machine fought against hundreds of Titans. The remaining forces of the keep, nearly a thousand strong, pressed behind the machine towards the docks. The city was to be abandoned, all that remained was the destruction of their enemy. Tengri flew high above, scouting enemy movements on the island, directing the Manticore to protect the armies. Lizard, Cat, Rat and Porcupine fought as well, dying by the dozens, as poisoned stingers and wicked mandibles struck into the fleeing soldiers. Tiamat's Crocodiles held back hundreds of Khepri at a time, as their bodies became covered in the creatures. Tengri would pick up and drop the harder shelled Erlik, letting the force of the fall do his work. Menmer would not reach the outer walls, an eight legged Khepri leapt from the walls onto the boy-king. Tydeus was stung in the shoulder by a Pazuzu and it was in turn slain upon his quills and yet the elderly Tyrant continued to fight on.

Though sealed outside the city, the Kraken rose from the ocean to attach to the docks. The vessel of Alexandreta, the Kraken had been built by its founders and the scientists who operated it timed their ascent perfectly. Its mechanical tentacles lashed out at the carapaced monsters, pulling the larger ones off injured soldiers. Its acidic spray melted masses of the creatures into the stonework. The beaked maw opened to let soldiers board it. When nearly a hundred soldiers had boarded, Rodenalus opened the hatch on the Manticore and pulled the other operator from within it. The two rushed toward the Kraken as the last surviving soldiers held off the Titans. There was no more room for anyone, as Rodenalus looked back as the beak closed, the last soldiers were overrun and the Titans made their way toward the docks. The Kraken released its grip on the docks and sank once again below the waves. Ninety soldiers, Hyperian and Khonshan, were crammed into the Kraken. Few were comfortable inside it, except for Tiamat, the only surviving crocodile. Every few hours, the ship would surface and check for Tengri, guiding the ship toward Lemuria. During the brief periods above water, many soldiers took the chance to walk along the upper decks.

A week of sailing brought them to Monthu. The Khonshan capital greeted the survivors with dismay. The riverlands of lower Khonshu were as yet safe from Khepri attacks. Indeed, Khonshan assaults had actually enslaved a number of the scarabs but with their Pharaoh dead, the kingdom had no leadership. The priests and advisers had no army to provide and so the Kraken and its soldiers were alone in their endeavor. Word had reached Monthu of a land mass that moved off the western cape, heading north. The ship took on supplies and set off north. If Lemuria reached Alexandreta, the hive would learn of their defeat and the Kraken would never find the Khepri 'capital'.

For a day the soldiers remained cramped in the confines of the submersible ship, balancing their fear between the crushing water and the crushing mandibles of their enemy. In the early hours on the second day out from Monthu, Tengri spotted the island whale. When the Kraken surfaced nearer to the creature, the smell of death and carrion filled the air. Tydeus, Tengri, Tiamat and Rodenalus and the other generals discussed their attack. The decision was to slay the Bahamutian. The creature had suffered enough and sinking Lemuria beneath the waves, would in turn, kill the hive. The Titan's sanctuary would become their tomb. Tengri said his farewells, a bird had no business below ground and he would be of no use to them. He flapped his wings and lifted off from the Kraken and flew off into the east.

Their attack was not expected. The tunnels of the whale were unguarded and the assault met no resistance until they were deep within the creature itself. What the Titans had done to this creature was monstrous. The attackers felt both revulsion and rage and when they came upon their first enemies, they routed them quickly. With their first battle done, the hive would soon realize that it was under attack. The fight became a running battle, as soldiers fell around them, Tydeus, Tiamat and Rodenalus tried to quicken their pace but the poisoned wound and the increased aged of the Tyrant slowed them. He repeatedly called *from them to press on but the other two saw in his eyes he wished to see this fight to the end, only then would his bones allow him to give up. Tiamat knew the pain the poison caused but her physiology allowed her to eventually overcome the Khepri poison, the aged Porcupine however, would eventually succumb. The skull of Lemuria had been bored through by the hive. As they entered the brain cavity, a hatchery lay before them. Rodenalus had brought flasks of Hyperian fire with him. It was with these ever-burning fires, that even water could not douse, that they planned to destroy the hive of the Titans. He threw them against the brain and the eggs, trying to lay an even amount. The oil had yet to be lit but his flint and tinder would end the war for good.*

Tydeus screamed in pain as Rodenalus tried to set the room aflame. Tiamat turned to see a long dagger-like arm piercing through Tydeus' chest. The Hyperian Tyrant was dead before the Khepri had flung him from its arm. A dozen smaller Khepri followed in behind it, blocking the passage out. Each of them had eggs strapped to their backs and with one horrible, chittering voice they spoke.

They spoke of doom, of death, of an age of giants and the fire that had destroyed it. They spoke of countless masses, of endless horrors, of an age of apes and the water that had destroyed it. They had survived it all and they would survive this. As they spoke, the Khepri slowly left through the tunnel. As each left, the voice became slowly unintelligible, as the sounds that Khepri could make were no longer spoken. When at last only the scythe-like monster remained, Rodenalus got his spark and the Hyperian fire trailed across the room, illuminating the face of the creature. As if a thousand maws had opened at once, it screamed and leapt at Tiamat.

The two fought, with blade and scythe, with carapace and scale. As the demon lord gained the upper hand, Rodenalus took advantage of an opening, the only chance an inventor would have and using Tydeus' sword, struck into the creature's leg. Tiamat opened her own maw and crushed her jaws down upon the creature's head. The monster's body fell away at the neck and the mouse and the crocodile were alone. Lemuria shook in pain, the tunnels flexed and bent as the two heroes stumbled towards the surface. The sea air stung their faces but their hearts were struck by the wreckage of the Kraken smashed to bits by the tail of the Bahamutian. The Titans that could not fly away swarmed the surface of the beast. The two quickly became surrounded. With their last efforts they fought off dozens of the creatures, until Lemuria dove beneath the waves, to die on the ocean's floor.

FALL OF THE RODENTIAN REPUBLIC

The original story of the founding of Rodentia follows on from The Rodeniad, telling of the two heroes washing up on the shores of the Mare-Civitas, far from their homes. Exhausted, the two set up camp and eventually a city, named after the two heroes, was founded where they had washed ashore.

Over time, the camaraderie the two had shown and the city that treated mammals and lizards alike, became a mammalian dominated Republic, where reptiles were slaves and the story was warped to that of two rats, Roden and T'ia, more fitting Rodentian names, as the heroic founders of the city.

This warped sense of history slowly corrupted the Senate of the Republic. Superiority of the mammals and particularly the rodents, came to be the core, of the Rodentian ideal, the aristocracy took advantage of 'lesser' species and eventually opportunism overtook speciesism.

Murius was one of the last 'good' senators, around the end of the Republic. Many of the other Senators had set themselves up as permanent aristocracy, taking from those whom they were supposed to serve. Although he had faith in the system and believed the corruption was not complete, Murius took precautions, gaining the allegiance of many of the military leaders of Rodentia. Murius did not believe a coup would solve the nation's problems but if his avenues of solution ended in his death, he wanted his vengeance to be total. After meeting with the entire Senate to place his evidence against the corrupt criminals in their midst, Murius disappeared. His allies, led by General Soricus executed their coup and destroyed the Senate, in the resulting panic, the entire city was burned and destroyed. The Rodentian Republic had lasted nearly 650 years.

Where Murius' body washed up on the coast of the island of Brisica, Soricus founded the city of Muriccio in honor of the senator. Soricus was crowned Caesar in March of that year and the Rodentian calendar was set to AF (After Foundation).

Timeline of Modern History

748 AF
- The Agamid tribe is defeated by Rodentian Soldiers. Scyzas and Lacerta are sold into slavery.

751 AF
- Scyzas is sold to Praetor Pyctoris, a Rodentian General. Scyzas is forces into gladiatorial combat, winning often for his owner. He is also taken along as a page, to handle Pyctoris' messages to the Emperor when far afield in wars.
- Pyctoris' forces are attacked by a horde of Hamsters, marking the beginning stages of the fall of the Rodentian Empire.

752 AF
- Scyzas escapes from Pyctoris during the retreat back across the Danidan River and begins his search for Lacerta.
- Scyzas finds her in Muriccio. The two flee east to escape into the Reptilian deserts.

753 AF
- Lacerta is slain on the shore of Lake Tiberias. Pyctoris is slain shortly after by a Chameleon.
- Scyzas, now free from slavery, vows to build a city for reptile refugees on the site of Lacerta's death; and names the city after her.
- The *Sultanate of Scyzantium* is founded and ruled by the Agamid Dynasty.

788 AF
- The Rodentian Empire falls from the combined might of corruption, failing economy and barbarians from the north.

810 AF
- The Felines of Axony take control of Agincourt on the coast of western Eutheria.

825 AF
- The City of Agaminople is founded and is made the capital of Scyzantium. Tunnels beneath the city are discovered that lead across the desert, including a path to Lacerta, allowing either city to be siege-proof.

890 AF
- The Great Mawenzi Empire of Zabar forms an alliance with the nomadic Monitors of the Varanid Tribe in the southern deserts.

945 AF
- The Holy Rodentian Empire is founded to quell the barbarian forces ravaging Eutheria under the Corelingian Dynasty.

1030 AF
- The Varanid Tribe completes its nomadic migration cycle and discovers Scyzantium in the northern deserts.
- Griseus, the leader of the Varanids, declares himself leader of Scyzantium.

1031 AF
- Deliberations between the Agamids and Varanids break down and war erupts.
- The Siege of Agaminople begins.

1035 AF
- With its link to Lacerta, Agaminople refuses to fall to the Varanid siege.
- Griseus discovers a pass through the Bayawak Mountains near the village of al-Karok
- Griseus creates a trade flow of Chugokan black powder from beyond the mountains.
- Using the explosive powder, Griseus is able to break through Agaminople's walls and end the siege.

- Griseus is crowned Varanus ibn Qutul, first sultan of the Varanid Dynasty.

1050 AF

- Varanus ibn Qutul begins to expand his empire, conquering the Hyperian mainland and northern Zabar.

1100 AF

- As the nation of Khonshu falls into the background on the world stage, it allies with Scyzantium in the hopes of accruing power.

1121 AF

- The Hyperians are able to take back part of their homeland. The lands East of Helios are still under Reptilian rule.

1289 AF

- Charles de Mange, last of the Corelingian Emperors dies, the Holy Rodentian Empire is divided amongst his four sons.
- Lowther, the oldest son, was given the coastal regions and islands of the Mare-Civitas, the Civil Sea. Lowther would continue this tradition and split his lands up amongst his own sons.
- Soripin, is given the area north of Lowther's, naming it Aquitar.
- Charles the White, the youngest son, is given The Western Vandalands.
- Ludwig, Charles' adopted son is given The Eastern Vandalands.

1292 AF

- Charles the White attempts to seize control of the Eastern Vandalands from his adopted brother.

1302 AF

- Charles the White surrenders to Ludwig, after a series of devastating battles fought against Ludwig's Kiwi Cavalry. Ludwig is crowned *Kaiser of the Vandalands*.

1350 AF

- Ludwig the Vandal, under pressure from the Nazarene Archbishop Peter Sylvilagus III, begins The First Crusade against the Reptiles.
- The Knightly Orders are founded out of desperation by mixed groups of soldiers from the Eutherian nations, as the war goes poorly for the mammals.

1428 AF

- The Northern Hamster Tribes migrate south into the Vandalands, bringing tales of giants from the East.
- Several Knightly Orders redirect their crusade from Scyzantium into the lands of the Ursal Khanate with great success. The First of the Northern Crusades capture the fjords along the northern coast of the Vandalands, before turning east.

1489 AF

- Vespucci de Ventura 'discovers' the continents of Vespuccia and Lorenzo de Muriccio claims it for Mare-Civitas.

1537 AF

- The Ursal Khanate strikes back at the Vandalands, cutting deep into their territory.
- The Gerbils of Federwerk, unable to fight against Bears, used their craftsmanship to build the Valkyr and turned the tide of the Ursal-Vandal war.

1528 AF
- Geckos from the city of Marluk in Bharat begin raiding the eastern coast of Scyzantium.
- Varanus IV forms a treaty with the Geckos and welcomes them into the Sultanate.

1610 AF
- Canines from the Vandalands, tired of being forced into Crusades, flee south to Zabar.

1672 AF
- Eque of Adwaita rides into Agaminople and proclaims the island's allegiance to Scyzantium.
- The city of New Muriccio is founded in Southern Vespuccia, a new city-state allied with the cities of the Mare-Civitas.

1682 AF
- The citizens of New Muriccio take in Capybara refugees, sparking the Civitas-Jaguero war. With the advantage of black powder weapons, the Civitans destroy the Jaguero Empire.

1700 AF
- Lacerta is seized by several Knightly Orders during the waning days of the 7th Southern Crusade. The tunnels are sealed by Assassins as they escape.

1721 AF
- Over mercenary crimes, A civil war breaks out between the Civitian city-states, eventually ending at the hands of Governor Hernan Pizarro of New Muriccio's armada. This places the colonial city-state of New Muriccio at the forefront of Civitan Politics.

1750 AF
- Varanus ibn Suley is crowned Sultan of Scyzantium, he makes Mwanza Kabir, a descendant of the Agamid Dynasty, his Vizier.

1755 AF
- The Knights Tiberias, a Civitan Knightly Order, is slaughtered in Lacerta by Scyzantine forces seeking to reclaim territories lost in the crusades. The underground tunnels are reopened to enter the inner keep.

1757 AF
- The 8th Southern Crusade Begins in retaliation for the sacking of Lacerta and the slaughter of the Tiberian Knights.
- The bulk of the Scyzantine forces move on to San Murino, a port city on the Mare-Civitas.
- The Knights Fusilier and Knights Bubonic retake Lacerta in the largest crusade army ever formed.

1758 AF
- The Siege of San Murino is broken by a force of 5,000 Knights led by George von Geissel. His actions allow him to join the Rat King, an honorary list of Bubonic Knights.

1762 AF
- The 8th Crusade sieges Agaminople.
- The siege is broken by a united force of Turtle Riders and Siege Tortoises travelling from the eastern coast.

1767 AF
- Miguel Ivara is given command of the first 'Man-O-War' class warship in the Civitan Armada. He names it *La Pereira*, as the ship is shaped like a pear. While the name is non-threatening, the ship is, with its 300 cannon arsenal.

1772 AF
- The 8th Southern Crusade Ends with Lacerta and al-Karok in Eutherian hands.

- The Knights Fusilier are disbanded as mounting debts cannot be paid.
- April 27th is declared Tiberias Day in honor of the fallen Knights.

1775 AF
- The Fifty Days War - Ex-Fusiliers from Aquitar raid several Civitan city-states.
- Fort Ste. Ermina, the ancient Fusilier Castle is taken by Venture Company in retaliation.

1785 AF
- Hyperia seeks reunification with Civitas, sending diplomats to the governors of each Civitan City-State. Their requests are largely ignored.

1779 AF
- T.C. Meles vanishes in the Aquitaran countryside.
- Meles of Burgunda is imprisoned for speaking against Shrouis XVI, King of Aquitar.
- Fellow soldiers of Meles, from St. Cyrien Academy, begin plotting to overthrow Shrouis XVI, forming the 'Union of Burgunda'.

1782 AF
- The Union of Burgunda's plot fails and Meles is executed in Palisade to a cheering crowd.

1783 AF
- A young Salah ad-Din Varanus ibn Suley reclaims Lacerta for Scyzantium with only a handful of Sand Guard and Chameleons. With instability in Aquitar and Civitas and the recent death of Kaiser Hedgehauser XV, no retaliation occurs.

1784 AF
- Hans Hedgehauser XVI is crowned the youngest Kaiser of The Vandalands. His ministers and regents become the de facto rulers of the country, keeping the boy-King unaware of outside occurrences.

1785 AF
- Louis De Bore, a nomadic mole, rallies the remaining members of the Union of Burgunda as 'The Claw of Malaise'.

1786 AF
- Arctos Nevsky is crowned Prince of Novagrad, a city on the border between the Ursal Khanate and the Vandalands. This city is often at war and the position is both one of respect and danger.

1787 AF
- The working class of Aquitar demands change in labor laws, their cries fall on deaf ears. A number of riots occur in industrial areas of major cities.

1788 AF
- The Claw of Malaise spreads the rumor that Shrouis' wife stated 'Let them eat cheese' in response to the labor issues and increasing famine.

1789 AF
- The ensuing revolution overthrows Shrouis XVI but at the loss of Louis de Bore.

1790 AF
- After a break in the alliance between Khonshu and Scyzantium, the Sultanate sends a punitive expedition to the nation. The Khonshans quickly surrenders and the country is made a principality of the Sultanate.
- Varanus ibn Suley gives his youngest hatchling, Elgavish, control over the new Principality of Khonshu.

1791 AF

- Louis de Bore is posthumously named Moleon the First, his adopted son, Jean de Claw, ascends the throne as Moleon II founding the *Empire of Aquitar.*

1792 AF

- George von Geissel, tired of the rule of regents and the corruption of the Knights Bubonic, cuts his knotted tail, resigning from the Rat King and the Knights. Though ex-communicated, George the Scourge forges an army of like minded citizens, known as the Dishonor Guard.

1793 AF

- The 'White Death' spreads throughout Ermindorf, capital of the Vandalands, thousands are infected and the infantry abandon the city. The Cavalry are forced to seal the city and kill any attempting to escape.

- Kaiser Hedgehauser learns of the rebellion and plague. Horrified at his regents' and ministers' mishandling of the situations, he expels them all from his court and takes control of his reign.

1794 AF

- The Hartnell Troughton Pertwee Medical Institute is founded in Ermindorf, in the hopes of furthering medical science to never let a disaster like the White Death occur again.

1798 AF

- The Dishonor Guard, after raiding and destroying dozens of Bubonic Castles, is folded into the King's Army and George is knighted for his actions 'opening the eyes of his kaiser'.

1799 AF

- Gotz von Federwerk recreates the Valkyr Corp. and designs the Mk.1 Iron Skinned Valkyr.

1802 AF

- Armando Reyas takes a Band of Lancers into Hyperia to help retake their lands from Scyzantium.

1803 AF

- To avoid war with the Federated States of Vespuccia, Moleon II sells Aquitar's territories on the mainland in the Shrouisiana Purchase. The Aquitaran Antilles off the coast of Vespuccia and the Aquitaran Multinsula islands in the Zealic Ocean are all that remain of Aquitar's colonial expansion.

1804 AF

- Juan Chamomile of Brisica and Princess Tetra of Hyperia disappear in the night. This sparks the Hyperian-Civitas War.

1805 AF

- The Hyperian-Citivas War - Enraged at the Civitan's betrayal, Tyrant Cypriot takes the entirety of the Hyperian Naval Armada to Brisica and begins the siege of Muriccio.

- The government of Muriccio, having no knowledge of the events between Juan and Tetra, agree to assist in the search of the missing princess and the impending rule of Hyperia.

- The Battle of the Ice - In an attempt to end Ursal raids, the Valkyr Corp. attack the city of Novagrad. Arctos leads the counter assault against the Valkyr Corp. across the frozen lake outside Novagrad. The combined weight of the Ursal and Valkyr forces is too great for the ice beneath them. Most of Novagrad's forces are lost to the lake and the Valkyr Corp, using mostly old, boyant, wood Valkyr, are able to take the city.

- Arctos is rescued by a tribe of Hamsters who believes him to be Wodin reborn. Arctos, suffering from amnesia, accepts his new position.

1806 AF

- Admiral Ivara of Civitas begins rallying the city states that have not fallen to Hyperian rule against the invading force. Quickly gathering an Armada equal in size to the Hyperian's.

1807 AF

- The Ursal Khanate reclaims Novagrad from The Vandalands using a joint force of Wolves and Bears.

1810 AF

- The failing physical and mental health of Moleon II leads to a series of communiques to attack Civitan Territories. The Civitans retaliate, ignoring, Moleon's regent and son, Charles de Bore's requests for a cease fire. This failure of communication begins the Aqui-Civitas War.

- The Island of Sardus is captured by Captain Rochambeau of the Aquitaran Navy.

1812 AF

- A 'Dragon' slaughters two battalions of Aquitaran Fusiliers and fifty Venture Company Mercenari in the city of Cordoba.

- The Aquitaran Foreign Legion is formed to combat these sorts of larger enemies.

- The Hyperian-Civitas War ends with the return of Juan and Tetra during the climactic battle in the harbor of Helios.

- The Skyguard's prototype airship crashes outside of Steinausderram.

1813 AF

- Axony's elite group known as 'The Experts' assault St. Cyrien with the assistance of Admiral Ivara and a small band of Civitan Marines.

- The Valkyr Corp., operating as mercenaries are on behalf of the Civitan City-states, lead Charles de Bore to attack Vandal territories, bringing the Vandals into the Aqui-Civitas War.

1815 AF

- Agaminople is moved south, to a more central part of the empire. Old Agaminople is renamed Iguabul.

- The Skyguard's first working airship, the Starkvind successfully flies.

- The Sons of Sardus retake their island home from Aquitaran control.

- Venture Company and Federwerk Industries begin working together, forming a trade agreement between the two nations.

- The 'White Death' reappears in the port city of Sikelia, Hyperia.

- The success of the trade agreement between Venture and Federwerk alienate the other city-states. Many place trade restrictions on each other.

1816 AF
- Moleon II dies of a stomach illness. His son, Charles de Bore, becomes Moleon III and takes full control of Aquitar.
- The Aqui-Civitas War ends with Moleon II's death and the supplication of Aquitar.

1817 AF
- Kit H. Flintlock, Admiral of the Aquitaran Navy is declared a traitor and banished. Admiral Jean-Vimeur de Rochambeau is made Admiral of the Fleet in his place.
- The *Bleu Septembre* is launched by Undermining Inc.'s development docks in Aquitaran Multinsula.

1818 AF
- The Skyguard becomes an independent group of Air Privateers but continue to operate for Vandal interests.
- Aquitar forms an alliance with Scyzantium to avoid extreme tax penalties placed on them by the Civitans and Vandals after the previous war. In return, Aquitar open's their shipyards and ports for Scyzantine use, expanding Scyzantium's fleet and Lemurian Ocean trade.
- The city of Lacerta becomes a dual-nation city, split between Scyzantium and Aquitar to foster trade between the peoples of the two nations.
- Salah ad-Din Varanus ibn Suley extends Scyzantium's borders into Mare-Civitas, taking San Murino as an official port city of the Sultanate.
- In fear of capture by the Scyzantines, the Civitan City-States begin forming a number of minor alliances, further restricting their international trade in the process.

1819 AF
- Admiral Ivara passes in his sleep aboard *La Pereira*.

1820 AF
- The second Starkvind is completed.
- The inhabitants of Bharat begin fleeing from 'daemons', seeking refuge in Scyzantium.
- Scyzantium will not allow the Bharatese Mammals to stay its lands. Elgavish, Prince of Khonshu, welcomes them into his principality.
- A series of aggressive and underhanded trade agreements, arranged by Muriccio, New Muriccio and Venture, forge the city-states of the Mare-Civitas into the **Civitan Trade Alliance**, a unified country with a single military.
- Venture Company, Sons of Sardus and 20 other Mercenary Groups sign the Condottieri Accords to allow legal operation in the Alliance. As a continuing independent state, Zapus and its Leaping Lancers do not sign the accord. **1821 AF**
- A group of Wolf soldiers from Novagrad discover Prince Nevsky is still alive and return him to Novagrad. He is eventually returned to his mental faculties, regaining his memories.

- Tamias of Venture travels to New Muriccio to investigate a string of gruesome murders.
- Tyrant Cypriot of Hyperia dies mysteriously, Prince Cadmus is crowned Tyrant of Hyperia.

1822 AF

- George von Geissel dies. His second in command, Leopold Kassel, takes up the title of von Geissel and becomes leader of the Dishonor Guard.

1824 AF

- The Wolves of Urssia, long under the rule of the Khanate, finally revolt against their ruling nobles in the Novembrist Revolution. The new regime, flush from its victory turns westward toward the Vandalands seeking to smite ancient enemies. In an odd alliance, the last Khanate city, Novagrad joins with the Knights Bubonic to defend the border from the full might of the Volk Ursal Republics and its endless army of lower class wolves and bears.

1825 AF

- The current year.
- Tyrant Cadmus banishes his sister Tetra from Hyperia, calling her a traitor and begins a war with Scyzantium. He intends to not just reclaim the last bit of Hyperian soil but to 'Grind the lizards into the Bayawak Mountains.'
- Required by treaty to pay for the post-war reconstruction of Civitas, the Aquitarans try to call in their debts from other nations. The central Vespuccian republic of Xalepena refuses to pay for the licenses and taxes that had been waved in the nearby Aquitaran Multinsula ports during the war. To reclaim the fees, to the tune of ten million Aquin, a joint force of Aquitarans, Civitans and Vandals blockade the nation. The Xalepaneans send blockade breakers out to meet the opposing ships and while the Civitans and Vandals back down, the Aquitarans sink the approaching ships, sparking the Maximillian Affair.

ORGANIZATIONS

Organizations are similar to *Legend* Cults but are not necessarily related to a religion or faith. Organizations follow a similar rank structure, being comprised of 5 ranks indicating the Adventurer's progression through the organization. While magic is not gained by progressing up the ranks, new items, tactical abilities, or favors may become available. Just like with Cults, an Adventurer may select an organization to become a part of without devoting POW to their Duty skill but any actual progression will require dedicated POW.

Increasing Rank

Each organization has its own requirements, after finding an organization you'd like your Adventurer to belong to, read up on the requirements for each rank, fulfilling these may not automatically entitle you to a rank up, especially if your Adventurer is out away from your organization. Promotions may require returning to the headquarters or local outpost of your organization to receive a promotion.

Exclusive Organizations

Some organizations are labeled as exclusive organizations. Such organizations will also denote a subtype, such as, military, technology, or religion.. Members of such organizations cannot hold Sergeant, Officer, or Commander ranks in any other exclusive organizations of that subtype if they are Sergeant rank or higher. All organizations indicate a subtype for the purposes of Tactical ability requirements but are not exclusive unless noted.

Equivalent Ranks to Cults

The terms listed are the generic terms for each rank, certain organizations may have their own terminology for each rank.

Common Member - Recruit - These members are only tangentially associated with the organization, either mercenary hires, passive worshippers, or raw recruits, none of whom who have passed initiation requirements. Recruits do not truly count as members of the organization and must be promoted to Private before gaining any benefits related to the organization.

Pious Member - Private - These members have passed the basic initiation rites or requirements to become a full member of the organization. Basic benefits of the organization are now available to them.

Fervent Member - Sergeant - The second rank within an organization. Rising to this rank requires more focused duty to the organization, including taking and completing missions. Failure to perform your duty can result in demotion.

High Priest - Officer - At this rank you now have partial control over the direction of the organization, what actions it takes and how it handles its holdings in the world. Such opinions are still controlled by the Commander of the organization.

High Lord - Commander - Few organizations have more than one Commander, who is the official head of the organization. Some organizations that consist of multiple sub-organizations (such as more than one cult of the same religion) may have a commander for each cult, or large organizations may have Sub-Commanders with the same official rank as the leader of the organization. Such Sub-Commanders are generally given specific tasks within the organization, either focusing on the commanding of a specific battalion or particular subject of research.

Common Missions/Plot Threads

Each organization has common activities that it requires of its members. Listed within each Organization is a set of example adventures/missions that Adventurers can be set upon by an organization. Some organizations prioritize missions more than others, while some simply require fulfillment of compulsions.

EXOMORPHISM
Exclusive Religion

The oldest recorded religion, Exomorphism is the modern title for the worship of exomorphs, previously known as Diabolism (Aquitar, Civitas and Vandalands), or Yazdanism (Scyzantium). Repeatedly through history, this ancient empire has supposedly risen from the depths of the earth in attempts to conquer. Millenia before the first endoskeletal civilizations, the Exomorphs dominated the world. Worshippers of Exomorphs believe in ushering in the end times, seeing the ancient 'demons' as a vehicle for the apocalypse. Of the few recorded contacts with Exomorphs, faith in Exomorphism has never saved a follower from the steely grip of exomorphic mandibles.

Key Facets of Exomorphism
Levi Alphonse, Heirophant of the Left-Paw Path

A Star-Nosed Mole, who's cult was forced to flee to Vespuccia after persecution in Eutheria. With the religious tolerance of the Federated States, a permanent organization has since grown there, the only stable and public cult of Exomorphism in the world. Since settling there he has returned to the old world on several missionary trips to attempt to convert new followers.

Organizational Structure

Outside the Federated States, Exomorphism is illegal and practicing it results in imprisonment if the police catch worshippers first, or mob executions if local villagers catch them. With such threats to their faith, worshippers organize small groups that worship in secret, often near supposed exomorphic locales, unexplained tunnels, sinkholes, or ancient ruins.

Religious Iconography

Demons - In ancient times exomorphs were feared as demons and such iconography depicted these creatures in monstrous forms, with such names as harpies, trolls, or djinn. Art of such creatures are often stolen from ruins to be worshipped by Exomorphists.

Great Lizards and Apes - Two previous empires destroyed by Exomorphs. Among Left-Paw Path followers, Exomorphs are seen as a force of nature, designed to rise and destroy empires and species that have spread beyond their intended borders. Among Right-Paw Path followers, the Exomorphs are a civilization unto themselves, building expansive cave systems beneath our feet, waiting for the time to conquer the world. In either case, evidence of Great Lizards and Ape nations are rare, fossil records of little reputation and even scarcer archaeological evidence.

The Hive - Exomorphs are believed to be a collection of species that work in tandem to achieve their goals, with lesser creatures controlled by their superiors. The Hive represents both this concept and the external forces that control our destinies.

Holidays - Many modern religious holidays are built atop those created by Exomorphists in ancient days. On such occasions Exomorphists preform their ancient ceremonies. The most important holiday is Insectalia, known in modern times as All Maws' Day, Hungry Demon Festival, Dios De Los Insectos and many other names around the world.

Ranks
Seeker (Recruit)
Requirements - Those that have happened upon a book in the library, or heard the ramblings of a travelling stranger and set themselves upon the trail of more exomorphic knowledge can call themselves Seekers. These 'followers' are lost, still seeking the truth. They have yet to find a cult, or have not completed the initiations with a cult they have found.

Acolyte (Private)
Requirements - Before being allowed to view the proceedings of a cult, a Seeker must prove their thirst for the end times. This usually comes in the form of a test, either to slay an outsider as proof of your conviction, stealing exomorphic artifacts from a museum or private collection, or surviving the depths of an exomorph hive. At least one point of POW must be dedicated at the completion of the initiation.

Rewards - Each Acolyte is given a piece of exomorph carapace or other relic to carry with them at all times, to remember that there are far worse things in the world than what they face in their daily lives. This item can take the form of a mandible, able to be used as a weapon, the top of the thorax, a handy shield, or any other body part, providing it is of some use and able to be hidden with relative ease (in a pack, under a cloak, etc.).

Compulsions - While outsiders may not instantly recognize the item for what it is, risking the exposure of the cult by flaunting it, or discussing exomorphs openly can result in severe punishment by the cult, or worse, by outsiders. Acolytes must also continue to hold their belief in expediting the end times, war and death reduce the world population, making the return of the exomorphs that much easier.

Zealot (Sergeant)

Requirements - To rise to the rank of Zealot, an Acolyte must uncover lost lore, gaining at least 50% in Lore (Exomorphism), Lore (Archaeology) and 3 other organizational skills. Additionally, an acolyte must have been a member of the cult for two years. As their 'initiation' they must hand copy the Maxilla Insectia from another Zealot's copy. At least 3 points of POW must be dedicated.

Rewards - A personal copy of Maxilla Insectia (Jaws of the Exomorph) a religious and research text bound in the skin of outsiders. While much of the book is filled, there is plenty of room for more detailed drawings and text. Time permitting, the Maxilla Insectia can be referenced to allow a reroll to Lore (Exomorphism) and Lore (Archaeology). It also allows Faith I to provide an additional Armor point to the Hit Location the book is nearest.

Compulsions - Zealots must pay 10% of their income to the cult, to fund research into hive locations and other activities of the cult.

Iatromantis (Officer)

Requirements - A Zealot wishing to become a healing seer, or 'Iatromantis' must focus on medical and scientific research. Raising their Lore (Exomorphism), First Aid and Healing skills and 2 other organizational skills to 80%. At least 5 points of POW must be dedicated.

Rewards - Many cults have patrons, hidden in plain sight, that give them access to cutting edge biological research. Cultivated toxins and poisons from exomorphs come into the possession of the Iatromantis.

Compulsions - Iatromantis experiment with altered states of consciousness, especially when it comes to toxins and poisons. Once a week, an Iatromantis must purposefully infect themselves with an exomorphic poison from their collection and experience its effects. Infecting others isn't a compulsion, its a hobby. Iatromantis must continue to pay 10% of their income to the cult.

Heirophant (Commander)

Requirements - A Zealot or Iatromantis that has survived within the cult for 10 years and raised Lore (Exomorphism) to 100% can attempt to become the Heirophant. By challenging the current Heirophant, the challenger will be drugged with the poisons of an Iatromantis and pitted against the Heirophant in combat. The Heirophant can also choose a second to fight in their place but the challenger must fight alone. Succeeding places the Zealot at the top rank of the cult and places all below them at their sway.

Rewards - Leadership of the cult, the fallen leader's Maxilla Insectia and the relic of leadership. The leadership relic varies from cult to cult but it is often a priceless artifact from the Exomorph civilization, recovered from Naraka, Uku Pacha, or Tartarus. The 10%

income from Zealots and Iatromantis fills the Heirophant's wallet and is used to pay back any Patrons of the cult.

Compulsions - The Heirophant must guide their followers on the path to destruction. The expedition of the end times and furtherance of knowledge of exomorphs is all that the Heirophant is devoted to; also that extra 10% income.

Organizational Skills
Evaluate, Influence, Culture(Any), Disguise, Language(Any), Lore(Any), Oratory, First Aid, Healing

Current Divisions and Commanders
Church of the Left-Paw Path - The dominant religion of the Federated States of Vespuccia, it has seen a recent resurgence in Eutheria due to the missionary work of its leader and a small cadre of followers.

Levi Alphonse - The Heirophant of the Left-Paw Pathists, this Star-nosed Mole has focused a large portion of his time on missionary work, traveling from the Federated States back to Eutheria, in the hopes of converting the old world population. As a visiting dignitary he is immune to conviction but has had little success in converting others.

Miskatonics - Less an exomorphic cult and more a label for those who believe in the existence of exomorphs but oppose them. While most simply see Exomorphists as insane cultists, Miskatonics see them as a threat to the world. In ancient times, the Jaguero Empire, The Bharatese Nations and the Hyperian-Khonshan Alliance were lead by Miskatonics. Since the fall of these nations and the white-wash of history, few Miskatonics are left to pose a threat.

Eutherian Miskatonics - These people know the truth and are a real threat to the continued existence of Exomorphist Cults.

Doge Tamias of Venture - During mercenary work in the Vespuccian Jungles, Tamias came upon the ruins of a Jaguero 'prison' for Exomorphs and barely survived.

Jean Cavernson - The CEO of Undermining Inc. has had a number of run-ins with Exomorphs, most often during the excavation of new Under-Housing projects. He does his best to keep his customers unaware of what used to live in their domiciles.

Wodinist Trollhunters - Hamster Trollhunters hunt exomorphs, or 'Trolls', for sport. The exact severity of the threat of Exomorphs is lost on Trollhunters but they share tales of their victories with anyone who will listen.

Ferdinand von Starkvind - A rare visitor to the Avian Kingdoms in the Bayawak Mountains, the stories of the ancient world and the Exomorphic menace have been shared with the airship inventor.

Hassan Kusuuf and the 11 Imams - The leaders of the Assassin's Guild travel the massive network of tunnels beneath the deserts of Scyzantium and are fully aware of the presence of Exomorphs. Sealing off tunnels systematically has kept them at bay and allowed the Assassins to continue to use the tunnels for their own objectives.

Common Missions/Plot Threads

Book Binding - Creating a personal copy of the Maxilla Insectia requires the pelts of outsiders. Each book must be bound in the skin of those slain by the Cult member. After two years of worship, this is a mandatory mission for Acolytes during their initiation as Zealots.

Mysteries - Learning about the ancient Exomorph empires and the ruins they left behind is the past-time of many Exomorphists. If a ruin has recently been uncovered by archaeologists (or just some poor sucker digging a well), Exomorphists are likely to be not too far behind. Rubbings of reliefs on temple walls, copying of texts and surviving exomorph attacks are some of the usual activities at such dig sites.

Tying Up Loose Ends - Each cult determines its own path to the end times. Some may see a certain organization, nation, or person standing in the way and focus their collective skills against them, in a secret war. Individual cultists may be sent to assassinate a target, politically ruin someone, or commit property damage. The exact means the cult uses is up to the fanaticism of the group's leader.

Speak to the Queen - Your cult believes the time has come, you and the rest of your cult believe you must start the end times by travelling into a hive and awakening a hive queen. Only the Heirophant knows if this mission is being undertaken (and the GM). The rest of the cult is in for a surprise when they find themselves surrounded by a swarm of angry exomorphs.

HARTNELL TROUGHTON PERTWEE
MEDICAL INSTITUTE
Medical

Brought together during the Ermindorf Plague Riots, Doctors Wilhelm Hartnell, Patricio Troughton and Jean Pertwee worked together saving the city from the Romero Virus (named after Patient Zero). While unable to discover a viable cure, they were able to create a vaccination to immunize the uninfected citizens. They realized, working together, they were able to press medical research beyond the usual slow processes and subsequently founded the HTP Medical Institute on the outskirts of Ermindorf. Since that time they have founded numerous campuses to encourage the sharing of medical knowledge across international borders.

Key Facets of the HTP Medical Institute
Wilhelm Hartnell

Born into a poor rat family in a small village on the southern end of Lake Ermine, Wilhelm spent his early years in the King's Army, finding a penchant for a medic's duties. After his retirement, he used his stipend to further his medical career, graduating from the University of Ermindorf with the highest honors. He then settled down to a medical practice for a number of years before the White Death came to the city and he found himself surrounded by rabid, violent, infected citizens.

Patricio Troughton

Raised in the city of Forjaz, Patricio was the son of a merchant and was schooled from an early age to become an educated citizen. Well equipped with his schooling, Patricio went to a number of schools, including the Universities of San Murino, Muriccio and Ermindorf. He holds a number of doctorates in Medicine and specializes in Virology. His passing friendship with Wilhelm brought him to Ermindorf to combat the plague.

Jean Pertwee

A Marmot noble from Strasbourg, Jean was educated at the Larrey School of Medicine at the University of Burgunda. He subsequently worked in the Aquitaran Army as a Military Surgeon. His family's marchland connections led to the request of his presence by Kaiser Hedgehauser to assist in helping the plague-stricken city of Ermindorf.

Doctorate

Completion of coursework at the HTP Medical Institute is not enough to earn your title as a Doctor. Showing ingenuity, tact and a focused career path to one's professors is vital to achieving a Doctorate with the school. Graduates are the most highly praised members of their fields.

Borderless Education

The Institute is one of the first open-border colleges, allowing members of any nation to attend, after of course passing the selection process. The Institute also encourages its graduates to spend time in other nations, as freelance medics, learning real life lessons about the condition of the world. Five separate campuses have been built since the first was founded in Ermindorf in 1794.

Ranks

Applicant (Recruit)

Requirements: An applicant to an HTP Institute, or any College, must send paperwork detailing their prior education, political and economic standing and other activities that prove their qualifications to pursue studies. Applications must be sent in for a acceptance for a particular fifth of the year, or semester.

Under-Graduate (Private)

Requirements: Lore (Medicine) 30%, Craft (Medicine) 30% and two additional Lore (Any) or Craft (Any) of 30%. Each school can only hold a number of students. You have a chance of being accepted equal to 5% plus 1% for each Lore or Craft % above the minimum requirements.

Rewards: Acceptance into a Campus of the Medical institute. Classes occur in Fifthly cycles for 2 months of the year. Participating in classes trains you in a subject based on a Teaching Skill of 50% and a Lore or Craft of 75%. For each skill over two skills you attempt to improve during a fifth you have an additional -10% penalty to your success (learning 5 Skills applies a -30% penalty to improving each skill). These cycles cost one step lower than normal training costs per skill you train in.

Compulsions: Continued enrollment requires successful training of half the skills you try to improve. Failure to improve or skipping more than one cycle removes you from the school roster and you will have to apply again to enter the school.

Post-Graduate (Sergeant)

Requirements: Completion of 12 Semesters (fifth year cycles) at the Medical Institute. First Aid 50%, Healing 50%

Rewards: A Bachelor's degree in Medical Science, A bonus to your Teaching Skill of 30% when teaching Lore (Medicine), Craft (Medicine), First Aid or Healing. At this level you can continue learning or find a job with any number of medical institutes in pharmacology, or as a medic in the military, +50% to your wages in such careers.

Compulsions: If you plan to continue post-graduate studies, you must follow the same compulsions as an under-graduate.

Professor (Officer)

Requirements: Completion of 24 Semesters at the Medical Institute. First Aid 100%, Healing 100%, Lore(Medicine) 100%, Craft(Medicine) 100%. You must prove your ingenuity to your teachers, by completing a dissertation or thesis on a subject of study you plan to pursue after obtaining your Doctorate. Spending a semester, with light coursework and enough time to write, will help you complete this document. Perform an appropriate Lore Skill Test and an Influence roll at the end of each week to determine if the content written is of appropriate quality. Each failed roll puts you back another week. Completion of 12 weeks of writing will create a thesis of significant quality to merit a Doctorate.

Rewards: Obtain your Doctorate in the selected field of study. This gives a bonus of 50% when teaching any non-physical skill. Your base wages in any field related to your doctorate provides +100% bonus to wages. If you gain a position at HTP, a stipend of 500 Gold Murin per year is provided for you to continue your research, teach in classes, or work in their hospitals.

Compulsions: Perform your duties as a doctor of medicine well, never harm a patient, or reveal their secrets. Any serious infraction of the Asclepian Oath may result in the revocation of your Doctorate.

Tenured Professor (Commander)

Requirements: After obtaining your Doctorate, the Medical Institute may hire you if your doctorate is in a unique field, or positions are open in regular fields. Working regularly for the Institute for at least 10 years, whether in the classroom, in a research facility, in field research, or in a hospital, Professors may find themselves up for tenureship. Such dignity is reserved for those that have proven themselves a value to the school.

Rewards: Tenureship. Except for gross misconduct against the students or faculty, your position and degree in the school can never be taken away. Your yearly stipend is increased to 750 Gold Murin.

Compulsions: The only compulsion for a Tenured Professor is to follow their research and never allow others to influence their work. The only way a Tenured professor can lose their position is through gross misconduct, or the absolution of their position entirely, usually due to financial constraints.

Organizational Skills
First Aid, Craft (Any), Healing, Lore (Any), Teaching

Current Commanders and Divisions
HTP Ermindorf - The first campus and largest, maintains nearly 3,000 students and continues to monitor the few surviving infected patients of the Plague Riots.

Wilhelm Hartnell - Wilhelm, the 'Rat Medic of Ermindorf' enjoyed a bit of celebrity status after his work in the Plague Riots, which has brought him into conflict with his colleagues due to his focus on 'big' medical issues, ones that will continue to bring him and the institution fame.

College at Helios - Founded after the village of Sikelia in Hyperia suffered an outbreak of a mutated version of the Romero Virus.

Patricio Troughton - Patricio's family of merchant mice has kept him comfortable in monetary concerns but he continues to throw himself into his research, seeking new cures and discoveries, never settling on his laurels.

HTP Wilder - A struggling campus on the Axon coast, the college is facing closure due to the information stranglehold of the Axon government.

Fiedler Gull - The twin brother of Lord Witney Gull, the Whitetemple Murderer, Fiedler has worked hard to bring his family out of the pall cast over his family's reputation. A pig in Fiedler's situation would find it difficult enough to win over the students on campus but his elusiveness and constant absence has led to rumors that Fiedler is no different from his brother.

New Orlea University - A joint project of the Federated States of Vespuccia and the HTP Institute, NOU has an expanded curriculum to non-medical based sciences, as well as math and engineering.

Jean Pertwee - Pertwee sees the current world of medical science as a travesty. Centuries of folklore and superstition sees more patients attending psychics and alchemists for magical cures. Jean has sought to expand the reputation of medical science, seeing his task to advertise a better image for modern medicine.

HTP Alexandreta - The reconstruction of the Island of Knowledge has been a steep hill for Hyperia and Khonshu. The HTP's intervention into their political issues helped continue the project forward and today the island of Alexandreta is a bastion for scientists the world over.

Sallah el-Kahir - A Jackal chemist and herbalist from Khonshu, Sallah is the foremost expert on pharmacology and his work in the lab and field research has jumped medicine forward several decades. As the Dean of the Alexandreta institute, he also devotes a portion of his time to bringing Khonshu and Hyperia back to the world stage, seeing the Island of Knowledge as the gateway for the two nations to prominence.

Common Missions/Plot Threads

Cram Session - Sometimes you have to work extra hard to finish your studies. Making some Persistence and Resilience rolls to boost your Learning rolls can help finish those courses. Maybe even make a few perception rolls to find more interesting or devious books of lore.

Field Research - Sometimes to really understand what you're learning about you have to go out and practice. Opening a clinic for the needy can be a great way to improve your skills and your status in town.

Quarantine - You never know when the next plague will spring up, or when a previous one will mutate. Expert students and their teachers may be called upon to assist in quelling a particularly virulent outbreak.

KNIGHTS BUBONIC
Exclusive Military, Exclusive Religion

As Nazarinity grew to be the dominant religion of Eutheria, the Church sought to reclaim the lands once theirs in the northern deserts, in the search to discover the site of Nazar. As the first Crusade began, thousands of soldiers followed their kings and bishops into the desert to fight the reptiles and there in a dozen cities, holding against the scaly hordes, they formed tight knit groups, which would eventually turn into the Knightly Orders. The largest of these became the Knights Bubonic, founded by Vandal soldiers. In the centuries since the first Crusade, a dozen other crusades have been fought, both against the Scyzantines and the Ursal invaders of the north. Founding several castle strongholds across the borders, the Knights Bubonic kept the Eutherian way of life safe from outsiders. In modern times they have been abandoned by their flock, who seek to dismantle the last Knightly Order.

Key Facets of The Knights Bubonic
The Grandmaster's Council

Since the disappearance of the Grandmaster decades ago, his Council has retained control, working together to defend Nazarinity. T.C. Meles, nicknamed 'The Thunder Count', was one of the most charismatic leaders of the Knights, he helped rebuild their forces after the 8th Southern Crusade took away so many lives. Unfortunately he disappeared in the Aquitaran Countryside while visiting a Bubonic Castle in the marchlands. His absence has placed the Knights in an uneasy position, facing increased political pressure to disband and the abandonment of many of their soldiers to the banner of The Dishonor Guard.

Turpin The Inquisitor

The leader of the Inquisition, the internal police of the Knights Bubonic, Turpin has expanded the Inquisition's duties to the citizens in Bubonic territories. It is also the Inquisitor's duties to perform clerical work and the general management of Knights' Castles. Turpin is the leader of the most extreme elements within the Knights, constantly struggling against Fierabras' place on the council. His official title is High Inquisitor.

Jacques of Martinique

Hailing from the destroyed Crusader City of Martinique, Jacques commands the Bubonic forces in the field having led them to a number of victories in the Aqui-Civitas War on the side of the Civitan-Vandal Alliance. Considered by many to be too young for his office, Jacques was promoted only days before T.C. Meles disappeared, resulting in a rough start to his term. His official title is Marshal of the Order.

Lady Bradamant

Wife of T.C. Meles, the last Grandmaster, Bradamant handles the smithing of weapons and armor for the Knights, ensuring her blacksmiths equip every Knight that goes into battle. She also personally crafts the weapons of the Council. Her official title is High Armorer of the Council.

Fierabras of the Wadi

A Monitor from the riverlands between San Murino and Agaminople, Fierabras is a convert to Nazarinity. Before his forces were defeated during the 8th Southern Crusade, Fierabras had a vision of the fall of Nazar and converted on the spot. Fierabras defended himself for nearly an hour, refusing to outright slay any Knight who fought him. Bradamant and Jacques came to his rescue and accepted his conversion. Fierabras would eventually rise to his position on the council by his understanding of Scyzantine politic and tactics. His official title is Deputy of the Grandmaster.

Bubonic Poison

Concocted during the Second Crusade, bubonic poison was used to some effect against Scyzantines, severely damaging the brain function of those affected by it. Work with toxins and diseases continues today in limited capacity, as the elimination of biological warfare is a subject many politicians, that opposed the Knights, used to gain leverage over the Kings and Dukes who allow the Knights to operate in their territories.

Religious Iconography

Nazarinity - The Knights follow an extreme form of Nazarinity and have much the same iconography as Orthodox Nazarenes, except the usually nondescript forms of the Shadow Army are shown as Scyzantine reptiles or Ursal bears and wolves.

Ranks
Rodent-At-Arms (Recruit)

Requirements: Citizens of the territories under Bubonic control are required to serve in the Forces of the Knights as Rodents-At-Arms (a title used even for those not truly rodent). Any follower of the Nazarene faith can also join the ranks of the Knights by finding a recruiter in Eutherian Capitals or major cities.

Knight-Errant(Private)

Requirements: Those that have dedicated at least 1 POW to Nazarinity and show a Combat Style and Duty (Nazarinity) of at least 30% can seek to join the Knights Bubonic.

Rewards: Swearing your allegiance to the Knights converts your dedicated POW and duty to Nazarinity to the Knights Bubonic. A mentor travels with you for a year, teaching you their skills and experiences.

Compulsions: A Knight-Errant must travel out into the world, seeing the current state of the world for a year's journey, accompanied by a Knight-Brother as their mentor. They must seek to right wrongs and live up to the ideals of Nazarinity.

Knight-Brother/Armorer/Hospitalier (Sergeant)

Requirements: After a year journey, a Knight-Errant must return to Castle Burz, or abandon their sworn duty to the Knights. Upon their return, the Knight-Errant is evaluated for a position in the Knights, the Armorers, or the Hospitaliers. One becomes a full Knight by proving their highest skill is a Combat Style or Brawn. One becomes an Armorer by having their highest skill be Craft or Engineering. One becomes a Hospitalier by having their highest skill be First Aid or Commerce. Ignore any other skills for determining career path. All Order members must swear an oath and dedicate 4 POW to the Knights Bubonic.

Rewards: The equipment of a Knight is provided for them, including weapons, armor and a Kiwi Steed. Armorers include both armorsmiths and the architects who design and build Bubonic strongholds, Each are paid for their services and are given the weapons and armor of a knight. Hospitaliers include both those in the medical service and managerial service. They operate together to handle the day-to-day management of the Knightly Order's holdings in the world. Such work pays the best in addition to equipping them as knights with weapons and armor. Each career is paid 100 Thaler a month. Hospitaliers are paid an additional 20 Thaler a month.

Compulsions: The Order comes first and the protection of it is the duty of all. Inquisitors look for those not performing their duties and those that are incompetent are seen as much as heretics as those that maliciously undermine the Order.

Komtur/Landsmeister/Inquisitor (Officer)

Requirements: Each career path must improve their appropriate skills and Duty (Knights Bubonic) to 80%. Dedicating 8 POW is also required.

Rewards: Knights promoted to Komtur are given command of about a hundred soldiers and during times of peace mange these knights with little oversight. Armorers promoted to Landsmeister are given control of a county and handle operation of their territory.

Hospitaliers promoted to Inquisitor are the internal police of the order, meting out justice to criminals in their ranks, as well as civilians living on Bubonic lands. Each career is paid 200 Thaler a month. Inquisitors are paid an additional 40 Thaler a month.

Compulsions: Continued faith in Nazarinity and duty to the Knights is required of Officers. Inquisitors are less likely to investigate Knights of this rank but is not unknown to happen.

Grandmaster's Council (Commander)

Requirements: There are five seats on the council of the Grandmaster, The Grandmaster, The High Inquisitor, The Deputy of the Grandmaster, The Marshal of the Order and The Armorer of the Council. All the seats are elected yearly but with the fate of the Grandmaster unknown, his seat remains empty until such time as he is found, or his fate learned. The Deputy is selected by vote of the other three council seats. The High Inquisitor is elected by the Inquisitors, the Armorer by the Landsmeisters and the Marshal by the Komtur. Normally the Grandmaster is elected by the entirety of the Komtur, Landsmeisters and Inquisitors. Taking a seat on the council requires the devotion of all POW to the Knights.

Rewards: A seat on the council pays 500 Thaler a month in addition to the powers granted to each seat. The Deputy has veto power over any discussion but no actual voting power in the council, he also commands the Rodent-at-Arms auxiliary forces in combat. The Marshal commands the Knight forces in combat but does not handle any of their upkeep. The Armorer equips the Knights and oversees construction of housing for the Order. The High Inquisitor polices the Order but has no right to accuse/prosecute other Council members, he also handles the managerial/clerical work of the Order, to ensure that funds are handled appropriately.

Compulsions: The Council only answers to the Grandmaster, who is missing. As such, little compulsion remains to the Council, each acts autonomously but this is not to say they may find their hands tied by each others political machinations.

Organizational Skills

Combat Style, Brawn, Craft, Engineering, First Aid, Commerce, Lore (Nazarinity), Culture (Nazarinity), Ride,

Current Divisions and Commanders

Castle Burz - The headquarters of the Knights Bubonic has stood for nearly eight hundred years. Burz lays in a secluded valley and began life as a monastery from which the monks took up arms to fight in the Crusades.

Marshal Jacques - Military Commander of the Knights, Jacques, a young mouse from the desert, has more experience than his age lets on. He finds himself constantly attempting to prove himself to the Inquisitors and his subordinates.

Lady Bradamant - Wife of the missing Grandmaster, Lady Bradamant has fought on the field of battle nearly as much as her husband. While not on crusade, This Badger works the forges, smithing weapons and armor for the Knights.

Tengriburg - A Bubonic holding in the Aquitaran side of the marchlands between Aquitar and Vandalands. This was originally a castle of the Knights Tiberias before they were destroyed at Lacerta. Tengriburg is the home of the Inquisition.

Inquisitor Turpin - Far away from most territories of the Knights, the Inquisitors are able to work in secret. The enterprising Rat has built a number of extra layers to the castle, performing scientific research beneath ground level.

al-Karok - A desert trade-city at the entrance to a pass through the Bayawak Mountains. This is the last holding of the crusaders in the Scyzantine deserts. The control of this city provides a decent monetary flow for the failing Knights.

Deputy Fierabras - With the constant conflicts between the Reptilian civilians and the Eutherian rulers, Fierabras was placed in command in an attempt to quell possible uprisings. Fierabras has done a excellent job of befriending the citizens of al-Karok, even getting some to join the Knights Bubonic.

Common Missions/Plot Threads

Expect It - Inquisitors are more like police than heretic torturers in the Knights Bubonic. They hunt down those that have committed crimes in Bubonic territories across the world, ignoring political borders. This does of course bring them into conflict with other nations security forces while in pursuit but the Inquisitors are generally effective at catching their target.

Vandal Order - The Knights have come to clash often with the Vandal Kings and their territory control, with the Dishonor Guard affecting the political landscape, the Knights are fighting a losing battle over their rightful lands. Keeping the Vandals from seizing their lands is key to keeping the Knights operating.

Crusading - The focus of the Knights is the defense of Eutheria, keeping invading Ursals and Scyzantines from overrunning the civilized world. Sometimes that means attacking first, to take and hold key locations along the borders. Such fights are often futile, resulting in martyrs more than real victories.

NATIONAL MILITARY
Exclusive Military
Each nation forms its own standing armies and navies to defend its borders. These may come in different variations but the basic structure is the same regardless of nation.

Key Facets of the National Militaries
The Grand Armee
Rebuilt after the revolution, the National army of Aquitar no longer promotes officers based on nobility but on actual merit. The Command Staff is made up of new, skilled Commanders and Veterans that had been exiled under the previous dynasty.

The Grand Armee is equipped with steel reinforced pads on their arms and shoulders. This extra protection is useful in tunneling tactics. High quality firearms are the pride of the Grand Armee.

Civitan Marines
Dozens of mercenary groups from the numerous city-states were folded into the new national army of the Civitan Trade Alliance. While there is still some conflict between these sub-groups, Admiral Doria has pushed her Officers hard to bring the mercenaries into unity.

Civitan Marines are equipped for light combat, focusing on boarding actions and sea to land assaults. As such their weaponry is usually pistols and one handed melee weapons. Marines are also trained in the use of Venturan weapons, mounting them to their ships.

The Sand Guard
The bodyguards of the Sultanate and nobility of Scyzantium, also form the army. The Sand Guard are equipped with the foremost weapons and armor and are trained as elite warriors rather than a mass of raw troops.

With their natural scaly armor, Sand Guard rarely equip heavier armor than chain. Additionally the higher ranks wield Shamshirs, a thin scimitar popular in the deserts. While hand held firearms are unpopular with Scyzantines, massive arrays of cannons are used extensively in their siege warfare.

King's Own Hussars
With the introduction of Kiwi birds to Vandalands by bizarre trade routes, mounted combat became the premier Combat Style of the Holy Rodentian Empire. In the centuries since, the Vandal kings have cultivated elite corps of 'Birdmen' soldiers trained in firearm or lance combat atop these bird steeds. The King's Own are also prided for their

expert avian breeding, producing some of the best steeds across the continent.

For the Light Cavalry Hussars wear little but their uniform, to keep their steed riding fast. Braces of pistols or Repeating Carbines are popular with these Cavalry so they can keep attacking without worry of reloading. Heavy Cavalry Hussars still wear plate armor and wield lances or large spears to skewer their opponents as they charge past them.

The Dishonor Guard

Formed as a group of rebels excommunicated by the Knights Bubonic, the Dishonor Guard swept across Eutheria drawing recruits from hundreds of territories. This rebel army, attempting to disarm the Knightly Orders would eventually Ally with and then be folded into, the Vandal army. The Dishonor Guard has become a nickname for the King's Own infantry, as opposed to the Hussar cavalry.

To show their excommunicated background, the Dishonor Guard wear Bird-shaped helmets in honor of Tengri. The weapons of the Dishonor Guard are motley at best. The sheer size of the army limits standardized equipment. Original Knights still wear their armor and weapons but change their tabards to that of the King's Army.

Ranks

Recruit

Requirements: To enlist in a National army an Adventurer must come from that nation or one of its colonies.

Private

Requirements: Eutherian Militaries have a month long training period for Recruits before being officially promoted to Private. Scyzantines are selected and raised from hatchlings to join the military. At least 4 Organizational skills and any Combat Style at 30% are required to complete training.

Rewards: A weapon appropriate to the Adventurers Combat Style, or the National army's common weapons and a uniform that adds 1 Armor to each Hit Location. Joining a National army also provides a monthly stipend of 2 Gold Solidus in the Sand Guard, 10 Aquin in the Grand Armee, 40 Thaler in the King's Own or Dishonor Guard, or 15 Gold Murin in the Civitan Marines.

Compulsions: Joining Eutherian Armies requires two years of service before a soldier can retire. Scyzantines must fulfill a ten year service to the Sultanate. During such times Soldiers have off-cycles of service, generally a week every two months but this can vary in wartime.

Sergeant

Requirements: Increase 4 Organizational skills and Heroic Command to 50% and dedicate 4 POW. A Soldier must have completed their first term of service before being eligible for Promotion (5 Years for Sand Guard).

Rewards: An increased monthly stipend of 4 Solidus, 20 Aquin, 80 Thaler, or 30 Gold Murin. Sergeants are also placed in more unique positions, either acting as Drill Sergeants, Executive Officers, or joining specialized detachments, such as cavalry or siege weapon teams.

Compulsions: Sergeants in addition to their increased responsibilities follow the same schedules as Privates.

Officer

Requirements: For all Nations increasing 4 Organizational Skills and Duty to 75% and dedicating 8 POW is a minimum requirement. To become an officer in the King's Own or Dishonor Guard, an Adventurer must come from Urban (Upper Class) background. Aquitarans must attend St. Cyrien Academy and complete the officer's training program to be promoted to Officer.

Rewards: An increased monthly stipend of 8 Solidus, 40 Aquin, 160 Thaler, or 60 Gold Murin. Additionally, during the Officer's off-cycle they receive a monthly stipend of 4 Solidus, 20 Aquin, 80 Thaler, or 30 Gold Murin. Officers are the Captains of Ships or Platoons, they manage marchland forts, or govern small colonial cities, these are the general positions awarded to a promoted soldier.

Compulsions: Officers have a different service term and schedule from Sergeants/Privates. They serve for terms of 5 Years in Eutheria (Same 10 Year schedule for Scyzantines). They are given two months off duty a year, during which they have no military responsibilities.

Commander

Requirements: An increase of Heroic Command, Duty and Influence and two additional Organizational Skills to 90% is required for promotion to Commander. Dedicating all available POW is also required. Scyzantines require at least 30 years in service to become a Commander.

Rewards: Reaching the rank of Commander rewards a parcel of land, generally a few hundred acres, in Eutheria. In Scyzantium, Officers promoted to Commander are given the noble title of Pasha and given rule of a castle or town. These are often in the border areas, to provide a military commander with skill to protect the area. Monthly stipend for their active and off-duty cycles are both 8 Solidus, 40 Aquin, 160 Thaler, or 60 Gold Murin. Commanders are also placed in command of entire battalions, or naval fleets.

Compulsions: Commanders enter the political stage in addition to the theater of war. Discussing strategy and conditions of the military with the civilian or royal leaders is a core part of a Commander's duty.

Organizational Skills

Combat Style(Any), Athletics, Brawn, Heroic Command, Battlefield Awareness, Ride, Shiphandling, Boating, Drive, Influence, Evade

Current Divisions and Commanders

Grand Armee

Army - Palisade, Aquitar - With the border changes of recent years, Palisade is extremely vulnerable to foreign attack and the Ground forces have been stationed to defend the capital.

Marshal Bel Neyette - A charismatic and confident Weasel, Neyette was a close friend of Moleon II but has come into conflict with his son over the direction of the nation and its army.

Navy - Ste Tortuge, Aquitaran Antilles - The colonial capital off the coast of Vespuccia in the Lemurian Ocean, Ste Tortuge has changed hands a number of times over the years since the discovery of Vespuccia. The city's weak defenses rely on a powerful navy to keep it secure.

Admiral Jean-Vimeur de Rochambeau - A Shrew noble, Jean-Vimeur weathered the revolution due to his family's holdings being in the Antilles, far from the politics of homeland Aquitar. When the Aqui-Civitas War broke out, Jean-Vimeur's ship La Rochette alone captured Sardus City in the opening days of the war, this and later naval actions harrying Civitan trade routes led to his promotion to Admiral.

Sand Guard

Army - Iguabul, Scyzantium - The old capital, Iguabul was once called Agaminople but when the capital moved further south, the name moved with it. Iguabul is perfectly placed that the army can move within a few days to any prominent area of Scyzantium, equi-distant from Agaminople and Lacerta.

General Resid al-Jazzar - After escaping from the underground slave markets, Resid, a Sand Lizard, returned home to Lacerta. His captors caught up to him in the markets and picking up a stray weapon, al-Jazzar slew every slaver. His skill at the young age of 12, impressed a local Sand Guard sergeant, who pressed his supervisors to enlist the hatchling in the army.

Navy - Aqabad, Scyzantium - A port along the eastern coast of Scyzantium, bordering the Bharatese Ocean, Aqabad is home to the largest Gecko population and along with them thousands of turtles and a few hundred siege tortoises.

Admiral Piyale Uluj Muezzinad - An Anole of Adwaita, Piyale was never paired with a Siege Tortoise but instead sought a life at sea. Spending a few years in piracy, The crew Muezzinad was apart of was eventually defeated and press ganged into naval service. The young sailor reformed his ways and devoted his life to the Scyzantine Navy.

Civitan Marines

Army - New Muriccio, South Vespuccia - The most powerful city-state and also the youngest, New Muriccio has dominated the political stage of Civitas since founded by Hernan Pizzaro in the opening years of Eutherian Colonialism.

Captain General Chequal Diez - A capybara born in the slums of New Muriccio, Chequal spent much of his military life as a political liason, protecting visiting dignitaries. After an encounter with Doge Tamias of Venture and the formation of the Trade Alliance, Chequal was quickly promoted to Captain General and commands the Civitan forces in their current conflicts with the New Jaguero Empire.

Navy - Forjaz, Civitas - The premier shipbuilding city of the Trade Alliance, Forjaz is home to the main fleet of the Civitan Navy. Forjazi ships are built large and armed with heavy and numerous cannons.

Admiral Andrea Doria - The daughter of the Doge of Sardus andrea fought against the standard position of females in Civitan Nobility, often clashing with her father's sensibilities and eventually enlisted in the Forjazi navy. Beyond her father's control, Doria became famous as one of the few 'Lady Officers' in Eutherian navies. When all the Civitan fleets were combined under the Trade Alliance, Doge Doria put forth his daughter's name as a candidate for admiralcy.

King's Own Hussars

Cavalry - Ermindorf, Vandalands - Cavalry is the pride of Vandal nobility and the Kaiser himself is a famed avian trainer and rider. To keep the pride of the King's army nearby, an entire stable and barracks was built into Castle Ermindorf, despite the strategic uselessness of cavalry within castle grounds.

Kaiser Hans Hedgehauser - Drawing his lineage back to Ludwig the Vandal, Hans Hedgehauser spent his early years in isolation, guarded from the plight of the outside world by his Regents. After the rebellion of the Dishonor Guard broke his illusion of the world and the state of the Vandals in it, the King took control of his reign and has made sweeping changes to the structure of the Vandalands.

Dishonor Guard

Infantry - Ermindorf, Vandalands - A number of outposts and forts in the vicinity of Ermindorf house the 'Dishonor Guard'. Once an army of rebels, seeking to depose the Knights Bubonic and return Hans to a place of power, the Dishonor Guard was folded into the infantry of the King's Army and their name was carried over. The small navy of the Vandalands is a subsection of the Dishonor Guard.

Lord Leopold Kassel the Scourge - A young farm hand who joined the Dishonor Guard while it was still a rebel army. Leopold was selected as squire to George von Giessel after his previous squire was killed. In the battles that followed, Leopold proved himself time and time again. When the Dishonor Guard became part of the King's Army, Leopold was given the rank of Brigadier but was eventually promoted to General. Leopold took the title of 'the Scourge' in honor of his late mentor, setting precedent for those that would follow.

Common Missions/Plot Threads

Training Drills - Keeping your skills in top shape is key for any military. Just be careful where you run your drills, failing to be aware of national borders, or civilian targets can be disastrous.

Special Operations - Sometimes a select few have the right know-how or tools for the job. Special Operations are usually secretive and stealth can be paramount for such missions. You wouldn't want enemy nations figuring out what you're doing.

All-out War - Sometimes communications fail, politicians refuse to back down, or a small accident erupts into a war between nations. Answer the call to arms and defend your nation!

NAZARINITY
Exclusive Religion

In the early days of the Rodentian Republic, when the foundations were still being laid, on the western edge of the Reptilian Deserts lay the city of Nazar. A rare city-state of desert mammals, they were mytholgically allied with the 'heavenly host', a group of protectors that kept the city safe from the nomadic reptiles. At the end of the Titanic Age, the heavenly host left the city, leaving the citizens defenseless. Tengri, the head of the host, promised the citizens that they would return in a year's time to come to their aid. Legend has it that after the host left the city, the Nazarenes we're left to fight an oncoming evil, a three month siege began at the end of their year alone. The evil that surrounded them sought to press on but the Nazarenes held control of the waterways that ran through the desert in those days, which have since dried up and leaving the Nazarenes in control would ruin their plans. Finally the day upon which Tengri would return came and the Nazarenes waited for his return, watching the horizon for the heavenly host. As the sun set the Nazarenes lost their faith and succumbed to the invading horde. As the ravening demons destroyed the city, the setting sun was eclipsed by a mass of winged creatures on the horizon. Tengri's forces returned moments late to save the city but in time to destroy the evil soldiers. This is the basic tale Nazarinity is based upon.

Key Facets of Nazarinity
Archbishop Petra XIV

The third female Archbishop of Nazarinity (14th use of Petrus/Petra as their Archbishopric name) Archbishop Petra was born Nicoleta Lepus in a remote Vandal county in the Bayawak mountains. She is generally considered more moderate or progressive than many of her predecessors and has assisted in the dismantlement of many of the Knightly Orders, long since an archaeic feature of the Nazarene political structure. As the Archbishop, Petra is the representative of the religion as a whole and sets the political and theological standards.

Nazarene Church

A small group of survivors from Nazar left before the siege began, sent to find help and warn others of the oncoming slaughter. The leader of this group was Petrus of Nazar and when he and his fellow citizens returned to the city with an army, they found the city had been destroyed, the only living thing in the destruction was Tengri, who wept before Petrus and his army. Without a word, Tengri flew into the sky and a sandstorm blew out of the south covering the city. The army returned to the west to share their story and few believed their outlandish tale at first. After spending nearly a century as an underground religion, just a few decades after the foundation of the Rodentian Empire, Nazarinity began sweeping Eutheria. Dozens of minor nobles changed their faiths and spread it to their subordinates. By 100 AF, Nazarinity was big enough to require its own central organization. The Nazarene Church rebuilt the city of Rodentia and created the religious capital of mammalkind. Since that time over two hundred Archbishops have dictated policy of Nazarinity, sending Eutheria to war with the Scyzantines and bringing them home again.

Organizational Structure

Beneath the Archbishop, who controls the city of Rodentia, are more than thirty bishops each stationed in major cities across Eutheria and beyond. Beneath the bishops are the priests and monks, who share and expand upon religious doctrine respectively. Lastly are the parishioners, some 75 million of them across Eutheria, with millions more of other denominations across the world.

Independency and Neutrality

Since its reconstruction of Rodentia, the Church of Nazarinity has been an independent state, on the modern border of Scyzantium and the Civitan Trade Alliance. Because of its proximity to the foreign and hostile nation, for nearly a thousand years the Nazarene Church used its power to organize armies to retake the Reptilian deserts in the hopes of discovering the original site of Nazar. With millions dead and both sides weakened, the Church finally gave up its crusades. As new Bishops, tired of war and political machinations, took positions, the Knightly Orders were dismantled and the Church became a neutral entity, seeking only to mandate religious doctrine, staying out of the political realm.

Nazarene Extremism

Some Nazarenes disagree with the moderate direction the Church has followed over the last century and a number of extremist groups continue to exist. The largest of the Knightly Orders, the Knights Bubonic continue to combat their assumed foes. The Nazar State Seperatists is a smaller group of theologians and archaeologists, crossing national borders and seizing territory to search for the city of Nazar.

Location of Nazar

The exact location of ancient Nazar is unknown. The rivers which ran near it, the Zab and Firat have been dry for centuries. It is the goal of some scholars and worshippers to rediscover the city, either for archaeological study, or for religious pilgrimage.

Religious Iconography

Nazar - A now mythical holy city in the western deserts. The original Nazarenes supposedly formed an alliance with 'the heavenly host', ancient guardians of the world, who saw the purity of the Nazarenes and believed it should be protected. The city is most often depicted as a door in the side of a mountain, split open with light shining from it.

Tengri - The leader of the Heavenly Host and protector of the good in the world. After a year long absence from the city of Nazar, Tengri and his army returned to destroy the shadow army. The phrase 'Tengri True' is a sort of expletive, invoking Tengri's promise and its fulfillment. Some scholars see a similarity between the Tengri of the Rodeniad and that of the Nazar story but most Nazarenes do not believe Tengri was an Avian, much of this comes from modern evidence of the known avians, such as the kiwi steeds and their inability to fly or communicate. Tengri is depicted as a rat with wings, holding a helmet shaped like a bird's head.

The Heavenly Host - A flying army that fights wars against evil across the world. For a time, they were based out of the city of Nazar, its mythically high cliffs perfect for their roosts. Most iconography shows members of the host as rats with wings, often wielding weapons and armor of the east, similar in design to Ursal Khanate, or the ancient Myo Clan of Chugoku.

Faith - On the last day of the siege of Nazar, the citizens lost faith and before night had even fallen, they had given up hope of overcoming their siege and fell to the invaders. Modern Nazarenes believe in the power of faith, promises and trust in a higher power.

The Shadow Army - A mysterious force out of the eastern desert that cut across the sands smiting towns and cities. Word came to Nazar that the army was heading towards them and their key position on the Zab and Firat rivers. The final goal of the Shadow Army, or Wave of Darkness, or a dozen other foreboding names, never came to light, as the heavenly host smote them within the city and left the city to the erosion and wastes of the desert. For centuries, the Nazar Church and the Knightly Orders saw the reptiles of Scyzantium as the Shadow Army, seeking to destroy mammalian life. Since the fall of the Knightly Orders and the selection of more moderate Archbishops, few Nazarenes see the Scyzantines in such a light but bigotry and a thousand years of fighting makes relationships difficult between mammals and reptiles.

Ranks

Observer (Recruit)

Requirements: Observing the holiday traditions of the Nazarenes is often the first start of many worshippers' Path to Nazar but the last stop on the way out for the faithless. Nazarene population is on the decline but many non-religious people still find observing the holidays an appropriate cultural trapping.

Parishioner (Private)

Requirements: Following the basic tenets of Nazarinity, performing morning prayers and attending services on Mondays, when able to, are the simple requirements of Nazarinity, belief and dedication of at least 1 POW shows true worship.

Rewards: Churches are always giving away copies of the Nazar Scriptures, a collection of works about the fall of Nazar and the years after. Additionally, many Churches are philanthropic and act like families within their communities, calling in favors while in your Parish results in a +10% Duty bonus.

Compulsions: Attending services where available weekly is a standard and paying alms is optional.

Priest/Monk (Sergeant)

Requirements: Becoming a true member of the church requires true devotion to the faith and a competent understanding of the holy scriptures. Becoming a Priest, who weekly provides sermons for parishioners requires Oratory 30%, Lore (Nazarene) 30%, Culture (Nazarene) 30% and Teach 30%. Becoming a member of a monastic order as a Monk or Nun requires Lore (Nazarene) 30%, Culture (Nazarene) 30%, Art 30% and Sing 30%. A total devotion of 4 POW is also required for either Priests or Monks.

Rewards: Priests performing services in their parish receive 25% of the weekly alms paid by their parishioners, while the rest is passed on to those above them. Monks have all their needs taken care of by the abbey that they reside in. Monks can also keep 10% of the money earned from the goods they sell, with the rest being spent on the upkeep of the abbey.

Compulsions: Priests must stay in good favor of their community and regularly perform services, such as baptisms, weddings and weekly sermons. Monks must stay in their abbeys for the duration of their sequestering, maintaining the grounds of the abbey, farming, illuminating manuscripts and other monastic duties. Both groups can find time to leave their duties to others on rare occasions, such as attending theological seminars, pilgrimages and missionary work.

Bishop/Friar (Officer)

Requirements: Showing 50% in the Priest skills with a devotion of 8 POW allows Priests to progress onto bishop-ship, handling a number of parishes across a country. Monks can become friars, by upgrading the Monk skills to 50% and devoting 8 POW. These ranks also require a Bishop or Friar's position to be empty.

Rewards: Bishops receive 25% of the alms paid by each parish (usually between 50 and 100 parishes) weekly but this amount is also for the maintenance and upgrade of the parishes in addition to his own pay. Each friar is the head of an abbey and determines what duties each monk performs and what special events the abbey will hold. The Friar receives 10% of the income made by the sell of goods from the abbey, such as illuminated manuscripts, farm-grown foods and religious crafts.

Compulsions: Bishops are often spokesmen for their region, offering advice to political leaders and to the world in general during times of hardship. It is their duty to keep the world's view of the Nazarene Church in a positive light. Friars are the true scholars of the Church, scouring through forgotten lore, copying ancient manuscripts and sharing that knowledge with the Church and their fellow religious scholars. They are able to continue doing this by proper handling of their abbey, managing the land's finances, food supplies and flow of religious material.

Archbishop (Commander)

Requirements: An 80% in all Priest and Monk skills and a maximum devotion of POW is required to become the Archibishop. Additionally, a Bishop or Friar must be nominated by at least two of their fellows and then voted in by the collective Bishops and Friars of the Nazarene Church.

Rewards: 50% of the alms of all Parishes and Dioceses of the Nazarene Church come to the Archbishop for the management of the Church and the city of Rodentia. The Archbishop also counts as Rank 1 in the following organizations for the purposes of Political favors: The Grand Armee, King's Own Hussars and Civitan Marines. The Archbishop counts as Rank 3 in Knights Bubonic for the purposes of Political Favors. The Archbishop counts as having dedicated the maximum amount of POW for those ranks.

Compulsions: Half the civilized world is your flock, while Archbishop-ship is usually for life, in times of extreme political or religious conflict, Anti-bishops have arisen as leaders of other denominations, often splitting the population of Nazarenes, reducing the income and political power of the Archbishop.

# Organizational Skills
Lore(Nazarene), Oratory, Influence, Culture(Nazarene), Teach, Art, Sing, Language(Nazarene)

Current Divisions and Commanders
Rodentia, Independent State of Nazarinity - Built on the ruins of the first Rodentian capital, the Independent State of Nazarinity lies on the current border between Scyzantium and Mare-Civitas. This coastal city is a major pilgrimage point for Nazarenes and near the center, Vates hill was renamed Tengrisus Hill, after the angelic icon of the Nazarene faith. On the hill is the House of Tengrisus, the residence of the Archbishop.

Archbishop Petra XIV - Her isolated childhood and time in a Nunnery, led the Hare that would become Petra XIV to be a quiet Archbishop. The majority of political or religious issues brought before her are usually met with silence, as the Archbishop believes in non-interference, as it is not her place to lord over the lives of others, only to guide. The only issue Petra has been vocal on is the Knights Bubonic and their rule over Vandal territories.

Common Missions/Plot Threads
Pilgrimage - The city of Rodentia lies on a political fault-line between the sometimes warring nations of Civitas and Scyzantium. In recent years this conflict has flared and it is unsafe for pilgrims to travel to Rodentia but this does not stop the faithful from making the journey.

Crusade - Although the Crusades are long over for any but the Knights Bubonic, the Church has found itself intervening into politics more than it likes. You could find yourself attempting to stop brinksmanship from embroiling the countryside in another war.

Missionary - Sharing the story of Nazar with the world is the duty of any good Nazarene and sometimes, as a missionary, you have to travel to new places and save the souls of those who live there. This is not the only duty of a theological missionary. Those with a skill in medicine are sent to help the oppressed and the educated are sent to teach modern knowledge.

The Empire of Aquitar

Recent History

Due to the aging and ailments of the late Emperor Moleon II, the Empire of Aquitar was nearly destroyed by its mishandling of the Aqui-Civitas War. The Regent and Son of the Emperor, Charles de Bore, was only just coming into his own on the political stage and was inexperienced. After the war came to a close with the passing of Moleon II, Charles de Bore was crowned Moleon III and spent the last 5 years reconstructing the country. Much of the emperor's power would be relinquished to Parliament separated between the Counts and the Marquis. The numerous Marquis of the marchland territories, were given equal power to the Counts of the Peerage, causing a political clash between the two levels of noble.

People of the Nation

Badgers

Ages ago, the reigning monarchs of Aquitar were the Melevingian Badgers, while fierce warriors, they were ill-equipped to be statesmen. In modern times, Badgers are looked upon as country bumpkins, or low-class workers. In the cities, many find work as Dock-hands, or in basic craftworks, having learned from an early age to use their size, strength and sharp claws to their benefit.

Gophers/Marmots

Originally from the city and county of Orlea, Gophers have a penchant for engineering and smithing. Gophers pioneered gun design and explosives, both in industry and helping find its place in the Aquitaran military. Marmots, an offshoot of Gopher, strayed from this stereotype, founding the continent's first hospitals and continue to explore the science of medicine.

Moles

Once merely nomads, with the rise of the Bore Clan to the throne of Aquitar, many moles have transformed themselves into merchants and nobles, forsaking their wandering pasts. Others are still on the outside looking in and those that did not raise themselves up during the Revolution are still treated as badly as any gypsy.

Mongeese

During Aquitar's early colonial days, under the Corelingian dynasty, Mongeese were inhabitants of Zabar and Khonshu, that were conscripted into the colonial armies. Centuries later, most have become naturalized but still act as outsiders, living the lives of loners, or in small groups on the outskirts of towns. They have also become a major criminal element, leading to the enlistment of many into the Aquitaran Foreign Legion, the only military that will accept convicts.

Shrews

The nobility of Aquitar, Shrews once ruled the kingdom under the Corelingians but now make up most of the Marquis. Having rebelled against the new Emperor upon his ascent to power, the Marchlands were slowly absorbed back into the Empire and until the recent war, had little influence in government. With the struggles facing the nation, a place in parliament was given to use the financial resources of the reclaimed Marches and amnesty to the few remaining rebels. Shrews are rare below the noble class but because of the wars, a few have lost their lands and turned to banditry, or mercenary work.

Weasels

The largest portion of the Aquitaran population, Weasels are common in all walks of life. The current Marshal of the Empire is a Weasel, as are a number of Counts in the Peerage. Recent industrial worker strikes were led by Weasels looking for additional hazard pay and many of the union busters were of the same species. Like their relatives, the Mongoose, Weasels also have a penchant for getting into trouble.

THE AQUITARAN FOREIGN LEGION
Military

During the waning years of Moleon II's reign, during the Aqui-Civitas War, an entire battalion of Aquitaran troops and Civitan mercenaries, at the city of Cordoba, disappeared. The lone survivor of the Aquitaran forces shared a tale with the Emperor of a horrible dragon, a slithering, scaled monster with golden eyes that consumed every soldier in the city. Although the Emperor's mind was failing and much of his duties were in the hands of his son, he still remembered the destruction of his own clan as a child and the terrible eyes that bored into his soul. Moleon II pressed his son for the creation of a new section of the army, a legion, that from the ground up would be trained to fight the larger, greater creatures of the world. Nicknamed 'The Snake Killers', the Aquitaran Foreign Legion was founded for this duty.

Key Facets of The AFL
Aquicois Bazaine

Exiled at the close of the Fifty Day's War, Bazaine spent the last few years of Shrouis XVI's reign on the island of Ste Tortue in the Aquitaran Antilles. Although much older by the time of the founding of the AFL, Aquicois Bazaine was still remembered by members of the Grand Armee and he was nominated for the position of Brigadier General of the Legion. His skills were far from rusty upon his return, having commanded the land security forces of the Aquitaran Antilles during his 36 year exile. His strict training regimen transformed his recruits into the premier fighting force of Aquitar.

Snake Killers

While dragon attacks are rare within the borders of Aquitar, their colonies and allies face much larger creatures than they do. As such, the Legion is trained to fight these monsters, often in dire circumstances. Legionnaires are experts in a variety of weapon styles, including firearms, melee skirmishing and even cavalry. Different combat styles are required to fight each of their opponents and Snake Killers are always ready.

Foreign Recruitment

During the close of the Aqui-Civitas War, troops were a valuable commodity and the newly formed Legion did not have the numbers to fill out their structure. As such, foreigners and criminals were allowed to join the Legion to complete their regiments. Eventually this became the standard recruitment policy for the AFL, with most soldiers being ex-convicts or foreigners. Citizenship for foreigners, or a pardon for criminals was presented to Legionnaires upon the completion of their service but strict training and regulations let only the best finishing boot camp, let alone survive their service stint.

Lacerta

The Aquitaran Quarter of the border city of Lacerta is the headquarters for the AFL. The Legion shares the city with the Scyzantine Sultanate, who possess the eastern half of the city. The peace and neutrality of both sectors has been on going since the inception of Aquitaran Empire, when the nations signed a non-aggression pact and absolution of the Knightly Orders within Aquitaran borders.

Organizational Structure

While the Non-commissioned soldiers may be criminals and foreigners, only Aquitaran citizens that have never been convicted of a crime may be officers. The total force of the Legion stands near ten thousand, with thirteen regiments. The Brigadier General commands all the regiments of the Legion, with Colonels commanding each regiment and Officers directing battalions within each regiment. Below that rank, soldiers may be of any citizenship or criminal status. While a soldier may apply for citizenship after at least 4 years of service, These soldiers are still never eligible for promotion beyond Sergeant.

Ranks

Recruit

Requirements - Entering boot camp for the Legion is relatively easy, even criminals and foreigners can join the AFL.

Private

Requirements - Completion of boot camp require at least 40% in 5 organizational skills and two months training. Dedicate 1 POW.

Rewards - Standard military equipment, along with desert wear and appropriate survival supplies. Aquitaran military pay begins at 25 Aquin a month.

Compulsions - Loyalty to the Legion, your past life is gone, those who abandon the Legion after bootcamp are considered traitors and are executed if caught. A minimum of a 2 year stint is required before a legionnaire is allowed to leave, or sign on again. Privates are allowed 2 weeks of leave each year.

Sergeant

Requirements - Finish two stints with the Legion and raise 5 organizational skills to 60%. Dedicate 3 POW.

Rewards - Allowed application for citizenship in Aquitar, increased military pay to 50 Aquin a month.

Compulsions - Sergeants are allowed one month leave each year but otherwise follow the same loyalty regulations as Privates. Additionally, a portion of the battalion is placed under your command, requiring your Heroic Command skill for bonuses during military actions. While off duty, making sure the soldiers behave is also the duty of a Sergeant.

Officer

Requirements - Proven competent in at least two military actions as a Sergeant and dedicate 5 POW. Only Soldiers who were previously Citizens of Aquitar before joining the legion and have never committed a crime against the nation may be promoted to Officer.

Rewards - Captains and Majors have the ear of the Commanders of the Legion and are able to influence battle tactics. Heroic Command applies a bonus 5% to the skills of soldiers under your command. Military pay increases to 75 Aquin a month and a small parcel of land is given upon retirement.

Compulsions - Officers may sign on for irregular service terms, shorter or longer than 2 years but have the same duty compulsions as Sergeants, including command of an entire battalion.

Commander

Requirements - At least 10 years service and increase of ALL organizational skills to 60%. There are a total of 13 Regiments with a Colonel each, along with the Command staff that make up this Rank, one of these positions must be available for promotion to occur. Dedicate 8 POW.

Rewards - Independent command of a regiment of the Legion. Increased pay to 150 Aquin a month and their parcel of land is increased in size and given immediately upon promotion.

Compulsions - Each Colonel reports directly to the Brigadier General but on the battlefield has direct tactical control of their regiment. Commanders have increased flexibility as to their loyalty regulations, able to take increased leave during times of peace but during times of war, the Commanders must remain at their posts.

Organizational Skills

Athletics, First Aid, Perception, Resilience, Ride, Survival, Track, Any 1H Combat Styles, Firearms Combat Style.

Current Divisions and Commanders

Aquitaran Quarter, Lacerta - The headquarters of the Legion is stationed in Lacerta and most of the Regiments are barracked within the city, or within a few miles. When on maneuvers or times of war, only a Regiment or two is left within the city and the others take up positions where needed on the warfront.

Aquicois Bazaine, Brigadier General of the Legion - A commander in the King's Army before the revolution, Bazaine was exiled by the King for losing a single battle in his 20 year career. Now a much older mongoose, Aquicois focuses on training Legionnaires to be their own commanders but in times of need, Bazaine has fought like his younger self, fierce and determined.

Taheete, Aquitaran Multinsula - The 8th and 9th Legionnaires provide marine security for the trade network based out of the coastal islands of the Zealic Ocean. Generally, this sub-group of Legionnaires is known as the 'Colonials' or Colonial Forces.

Yvonne Bougainville, Colonel of the 8th Artillery Regiment - Commander of the naval forces of the Colonials, Bougainville is a Aquitaran born Gecko, her parents having travelled much farther from Marluk than most Gecko refugees. Her last name is the Aquitaranization of the Bharatese name Bhargavi.

Jean Danjou, Colonel of the 9th Light Regiment - Commander of the marine and ground forces of the Colonials, Danjou is a Vespuccian Badger from New Orlea. After the sale of Aquitaran Vespuccia to the Federated States, Jean Danjou signed up for the Legion to return to his native country. Ironically he now lives and works thousands of miles from his homeland.

Common Missions/Plot Threads

To the Man! - Legionnaires get the worst assignments. Outnumbered and ordered to hold their positions, they are expected to die to the man. More often than naught though, they prove their commanders wrong and win the day against insurmountable odds.

Desert Life - Few supplies come down the line from the Grand Armee and the Legion is expected to see after its own, whether that be farming, construction, or executing deserters.

Espirit de Corpse - While Legionnaires may complete their objectives, the death rate of new recruits is incredibly high. Veterans are often the only ones left to clean up after a battle and in the desert, corpses can attract all sorts, from scavengers, to the types of creatures the Legion was created to fight.

St. Cyrien Academy
Military

Aquitar's premier military academy, some of the greatest tactical minds have studied, taught or visited the school. While until recently, only Aquitaran citizens were allowed to enroll at the Academy proper, the surrounding city has been the site of enlightenment and open forum, with members of any country coming to share in the off-campus training.

Key Facets of St. Cyrien Academy
Dean Fontainebleau

Philip Fontainebleau, a noble Marmot from central Aquitar, has been head of St. Cyrien since 1803. A graduate from the school, Philip held the rank of Marshal of Aquitar until retiring from the army at the turn of the century. He was then offered the position as Dean and accepted the offer when he found civilian life boring. Since that time Fontainebleau has taught thousands of students how to lead as an officer.

Famous Alumni

Meles of Burgunda - Brother of Bubonic Grandmaster T.C. Meles, Meles of Burgunda was the Marshal of Aquitar under King Shrouis, before being imprisoned and executed for refusing to give his soldiers suicidal commands. A number of fellow alumni formed the 'Union of Burgunda' in an attempt to free him before his execution but when their attempted failed, the organization became the Claw of Malaise and led to the overthrow of the monarchy.

Aquicois Bazaine - The Captain in charge of the force sent to back up the bandits in control of Fort Ste Ermina during the Fifty Day's War, Aquicois was exiled for his failure, the first in his career. After his return from exile in 1812, Aquicois was placed in command of the Aquitaran Foreign Legion and put his time at St Cyrien to work, training the Legionnaires.

Assault on St Cyrien

In a temporary alliance with the Civitan States, the Protectorate of Axony supplied ships and guns to Admiral Ivara, recently home from the exhausting Hyperian War, to fight their new opponent, the Aquitarans in the Aqui-Civitas War. Secreted in the hold of one of the Axon ships, the elite espionage group 'The Experts' stole into St Cyrien during Ivara's assault on the city. While the military might of Aquitar in the city dealt with the Civitans, the Experts snuck into the underground passages of the Academy proper and extracted a number of unknown artifacts. What they found has yet to be revealed to the outside world.

Open to International Students

After the War, Aquitar was forced to sign a number of treaties supplicating before the Civitans. The one requirement of the Axons in their treaties was the opening of St. Cyrien to international cadets and teachers. Aquitaran politicians, threatened with the secrets beneath the school, were forced to acquiesce and today, Civitans, Scyzantines, Vespuccians, Ribenguans and most nations now have students that study along side Aquitarans at the academy.

College of Infantry and Firearms

The Aquitaran school of tactics focuses on numbers and quality firearms. In wars that stretch across thousands of miles, you cannot always have the best soldiers or commanders at any battlefront. As such, quality manufacturing and simple, drilled maneuvers can carry any army.

College of Armor and Cavalry

Even with Firearms cutting through most armor, Cavalry are still a fearsome opponent on the battlefield. Elite soldiers cutting a swath through the enemy is demoralizing and devastating. The Vandals pride themselves on this strategy and their crafted armor and specially bred kiwi steeds are proof of that.

College of Navigation and Navy

Civitan strategy is based around their homeland and much of that 'land' is covered in water. Sailing is core to Civitan life and Naval combat keeps their ports safe and their merchants trading. Many of the mercenary groups of the Civitans were small navies and with most being folded into the Civitan Marines, it is about time they received proper training.

College of Cannon and Artillery

Scyzantium loves its big guns. In the ancient days of the Crusades, as the immortal city of Agaminople brushed off sieges, citizens would gather on the parapets or their houses and watch as cannons bombarded the city walls. Today Scyzantine cannons are strapped to tortoises creating the first mobile artillery. Of course, other explosives are also used to take down smaller walls and combat engineers and sappers are a vital part of Scyzantine siege tactics.

College of Scouting and Espionage

The island nation of Axony lives as a near police state. Every crime is investigated to the detriment of civil rights. Espionage is a favorite tool of the Protectorate and on the battlefield, scouting is an alternative form. Knowledge is as key to victory as any weapon and knowing precise numbers and army makeup can help you strategize and design the perfect plan to defeat your opponent.

Ranks

Applicant (Recruit)

Requirements: Students who already completed an undergraduate degree and/or have graduated from a University may apply. Students take exams on general knowledge, aptitude and intelligence; sit for an interview and pass a test of physical ability.

Cadet (Private)

Requirements: Athletics 50%, Brawn 50%, Any 3 Lore 50%, a total non-dedicated POW of 8 or higher. St. Cyrien can only take a few hundred students in a training cycle. You have a chance of being accepted equal to 25% plus 1% for each Lore % above the minimum requirements.

Rewards: Acceptance into one of St. Cyrien's Colleges. Each has a different set of organizational skills they will train you in and that are required for graduation. Classes occur in fifthly cycles for 3 months of the year. Participating in classes trains you in a subject based on a Teaching Skill of 50% and a Skill of 75%. For each skill over two you attempt to improve during a fifth you have an additional -10% penalty to your success (learning 5 Skills applies a -30% penalty to improving each skill). These cycles cost one step lower than normal training costs per skill you train in.

Compulsions: Continued enrollment requires successful training of half the skills you try to improve. Failure to improve or skipping more than one cycle removes you from the school roster and you cannot apply again to the same college.

Graduate (Sergeant)

Requirements: 4 Organizational skills of the appropriate college at 80%. Completed at least 6 cycles of classes.

Rewards: You complete the officer's training course and may immediately apply to Officer Rank of your nation's or college's nation's military, skipping private and sergeant, if you meet all the requirements. Additionally, you add double your Heroic Command critical range to the college organizational skills of soldiers under your command in battle. If you decide to continue studying at St. Cyrien, you may take another College expanding your organizational skills.

Compulsions: After graduation there are no further compulsions from St. Cyrien, unless you decide to stay on and further your tactician's career at the school.

Tactician (Officer)

Requirements: 8 Organizational skills from two colleges at 100%, Completion of 12 cycles of classes. Dedicate 5 POW.

Rewards: You may immediately apply to the Commander Rank of your nation's military or the Officer Rank of any Exclusive Military to which you meet all other skill requirements. Additionally, you may apply double your Heroic Command critical range to both college organizational skills. POW dedicated to St. Cyrien also applies to the military organization you join afterwards. Continuing education allows you to study from all colleges.

Compulsions: Cyrien Tacticians are prominent members of the school and reprehensible actions in addition to showing poorly on the school, also revoke your certification, resulting in demotion to Sergeant at the very least and discharge at the worst.

Master Tactician (Commander)

Requirements: Teach 50%, 12 Organization skills from all colleges 120%, Completion of 24 cycles. Dedicate all POW.

Rewards: You may immediately apply to Commander Rank of any nation's military or Commander rank of any Exclusive Military to which you meet all other skill requirements. Your Heroic Command critical range applies to officers below you, even if you are not commanding battles they participate in.

Compulsions: Attaining Master Tactician certification requires you to also teach at the school for at least one cycle a year. Such work pays 75 Aquin per cycle.

Organizational Skills

College of Infantry and Firearms

Combat Style (Firearms), Battlefield Awareness, Heroic Command, Perception, Influence, Evade

College of Armor and Cavalry

Combat Style (Any Melee), Ride, Drive, Evade, Heroic Command, Battlefield Awareness, Resilience

College of Navigation and Navy

Boating, Shiphandling, Craft, Swim, Track, Survival, Perception, Battlefield Awareness, Heroic Command

College of Cannon and Siege

Combat Style(Any Artillery), Engineering, Mechanisms, Drive, Craft (Any), Battlefield Awareness, Heroic Command

College of Scouting and Espionage
Stealth, Perception, Disguise, Sleight, Influence, Insight, Evade, Track, Survival, Streetwise, Seduction, Culture (Any), Persistence

Current Divisions and Commanders
College of Infantry and Firearms
The Badger in the Iron Claws - An unnamed prisoner discovered in the depths of Palisade Prison during the revolution, this badger is known as 'Iron Claws' for the paw encapsulating manacles welded to him. For unknown reasons, he refuses to speak to anyone except his long-time cell mate, Alexandre Dauger, a weasel criminal who turned his life around after meeting Iron Claws and being freed from prison. Alexandre 'translates' for Iron Claws, sharing his opinions and tactical strategies. The two fought together against the Civitans during the Assault on St. Cyrien. According to Alexandre, Iron Claws had no idea what had been hidden beneath the Academy.

College of Armor and Cavalry
Franz Kozietulski - A Shrew hussar from the Rivermark and professional Avian trainer. Franz sees cavalry as a lost art, with the firearm dominating army strategy. Kozietulski has focused on adapting cavalry to this new dynamic, focusing on light cavalry, able to sweep over infantry must faster than classic heavy cavalry.

College of Navigation and Navy
Camila Ivara - Daugther of Miguel Ivara, Camila continues the Ivara's naval lineage. Like her father, Camila is an expert in boarding actions and ship-to-ship combat, teaching Captains how to use their crew's strength to overcome ship-of-the-line barrage style warfare and even the fight with close quarters fighting.

College of Cannon and Siege
Seshata - A Leopard from Khonshu, Seshata was selected by the Scyzantine Sultan to represent the nation at St. Cyrien after the Aqui-Scyzantine alliance was cemented. As a master of siege warfare, Seshata designed many of the modern cannons used in the southern and eastern regions of the world. Coming from an architecture and engineering background, she teaches pinpoint precision and effective sapping techniques to combat engineers.

College of Scouting and Espionage

Sidney Page - A self-taught investigator and expert spy, Sidney is a Beagle that hails from the Protectorate of Axony. Although often missing from school grounds, Page's extensive experience as a crime sleuth provides him a unique perspective on the tactics of Scouts and Espionage. Detailing how many murderers and spies are caught, Sidney teaches scouts how to cover their tracks and stay alive.

Common Missions/Plot Threads

Beneath the School - What did the Experts find beneath the school? Why is Aquitar so willing to let foreign enemies train along side their own tacticians? Whatever is or was down there must have been amazing, or terrible.

House Rivalry - So many cultures and national tensions can result in healthy, or unhealthy competition. Most students join the College of their nation to feel more 'at home' while in class. This separation creates a great deal of rivalry that is just waiting to erupt.

UNDERMING INC.
Exclusive Technology

Aquitar's answer to Venture Company and Federwerk Industries. Undermining Incorporated is famous for its 'outside the box' style thinking. Its advancements today include Underground housing, Submersible ships and alternative weapon propellants. UI is seen as something of a laughing stock amongst the more Respected scientific development firms for its development process but its results are nothing to be ignored.

Key Facets of Undermining Inc.
Jean Cavernson

Owner and Founder of Undermining Inc., This enterprising Gopher built the company from nothing in just under 5 years, officially displaying his first company project, the Potato Gun, in 1807.

Potato Gun

This less than lethal weapon became popular with Riot Control during Plague outbreaks, as well as recreational entertainment. The basic hydraulic principals behind the device however, caught the eye of financial backers, who set UI to work designing more practical applications.

Bleu Septembre

More advanced air hydraulics were produced which led to the construction of the *Bleu Septembre*, a submersible ship, able to avoid enemy blockades and launch attacks without detection. This project truly placed Undermining Inc on the world stage and while the idea of a submersible ship seemed a fanciful machine out of legend, the **Septembre** has proved its effectiveness in skirmishes with the Ribenguan navy half a dozen times, easily outclassing their best battleships.

Bumbling *Blaireau*

Following on from their submersible success, UI designed the *Blaireau* a digging vehicle, designed to carve out tunnels either for excavation purposes or for military tunneling, to dig under castle walls. Nicknamed the *Bumbling Blaireau*, the prototype was working for less than ten minutes when it breached a sea wall. Never intended to be introduced to water, the vehicle was crushed by the pressure.

Under-Housing™

In need of a new breakthrough, Cavernson and his company continued with their minds on the ground. Using their hydraulic technology to cycle air through underground mines and caves, they were able to begin excavating safely, without the worry of toxic fumes. Their air recycling worked so well, they were able to make comfortable, affordable, underground housing so that nearly any citizen could own a decent sized property. The system was approved for a test run in 1811 and after the entire block under Palisade's luxurious Concorde Park was sold, A dozen more Under-Housing blocks were constructed, several outside of Palisade, in other crowded Aquitaran cities. While the *Bleu Septembre* is Undermining Inc's more famous development, Under-Housing has done more for the lower class than any other city development since the development of the sewer system.

Ranks

Applicant (Recruit)

Requirements: Undermining Inc requires a lot of employees, mostly laborers to keep its construction projects going. Any menial worker can find employment at the company.

Intern/Matelot (Private)

Requirements - An Internship at one of UI's construction sites, or signing on as a Matelot aboard the Bleu Septembre requires a Mechanism and Engineering skill of 30%. Signing up for the Bleu Septembre also requires the honorable completion of a two year stint in the Aquitaran Navy.

Rewards - Placement in either an Internship or a position aboard the Bleu Septembre once placed in either career path, cannot change to the other. Interns make no money but have their room and board paid for in a UI Under-Housing complex. Matelots make 10 Aquin a month.

Compulsions - Undermining Inc is a business, competency matters over political opinion or actions outside of work. Aboard the Bleu Septembre, the ship operates in 2 month cycles, switching out crew in the Aquitaran Multinsular islands at the end of two months. providing two months of vacation (unpaid of course) for sailors.

Lab Technician/Ensign (Sergeant)

Requirements - Successful completion of a one year Internship allows the Intern to apply for a Lab Technician position. An Intern must show Mechanism, Engineering and at least 1 other skill at 50% and have presented an effective design to their superiors. Those who have completed the officer's training at St. Cyrien Academy are automatically accepted as an Ensign aboard the Bleu Septembre. Matalots may follow an accelerated officer's program in the Multinsular isles during their off-cycles displaying Mechanism, Engineering and Heroic Command to 50%.

Rewards - A monthly stipend for Lab Technicians of 25 Aquin and 10 Aquin for each effective design submitted. Ensigns receive a 50 Aquin stipend.

Compulsions - Poor design work, or a lack of submitted designs might see the demotion of a Lab Tech. Ensigns must relay the commands of their superiors to their non-commissioned subordinates. Ensigns follow the same two month cycle as Matalots.

Project Lead/Submersible Captain (Officer)

Requirements - Promotion to Project Lead requires Mechanism, Engineering and two other organizational skills at 80%. The Captain of the Bleu Septembre must increase their Mechanism, Engineering, Heroic Command and Shiphandling to 75%.

Rewards - Direct control of project selection and a workshop and increased stipend of 100 Aquin, with a continual 200 Aquin for completed projects by Project Leads. The Ship's Captain has direct tactical control over the submersible able to determine what actions she will undertake.

Compulsions - Undermining Inc is driven by profit. Projects that are unmarketable, or simply don't work is lost revenue for the stockholders. Project Leads should avoid such pitfalls and build a team that can bring important innovations to the people. The Captain of the Bleu Septembre and his actions are watched by the Emperor and the high command. Veritably the flag ship of the Aquitaran Navy, any embarrassment caused by the ship reflects both on Undermining and on the nation as a whole.

Chief Executive Officer (Commander)

Requirements: Jean Cavernson is young, ambitious and to quote his last keynote address 'Just getting started!' Of course, as UI is a publicly traded company, the board of directors could drop him any moment (and then regret it a few years later and re-hire him). To get this prestigious position you'd have to prove more valuable to the company and its shareholders than Cavernson is.

Rewards: A stipend of 1,000 Aquin a month, Basic direction of the company and choice of projects the company will pursue.

Compulsions: Keeping this Job will be as difficult as it was to get Cavernson out in the first place. The shareholders will be watching your every move, especially when it comes time for the payment of dividends.

Organizational Skills

Swim, Commerce, Engineering, Mechanisms, Shiphandling

Current Divisions and Commanders

Under-Housing Complex 01, Palisade, Aquitar - The first Under-Housing project is now home to nearly two hundred Aquitarans, with Complexes 02-05 Home to over a thousand. Undermining Inc moved its headquarters underground into 01 after underground living became fashionable with the upper class, leaving the lower class to live on the surface.

Jean Cavernson - A completely unknown gopher until his company debuted its first project. Cavernson has been an elusive CEO, mainly speaking enthusiastically during press conferences and then disappearing back into the lab.

'They say great science is built on the shoulders of giants - not here. At Undermining Inc. we do all our science from scratch; no paw holding.'

Taheete, Aquitaran Multinsula - The dockyards of Taheete are home to the largest portion of the Aquitaran Navy, just ahead of the Ste. Tortuge flotilla in the Aquitaran Antilles.

Captain Ral Doré - A Badger naval officer before being assigned to the launch of the Bleu Septembre, Ral works in conjunction with the Colonial Forces in the Zealic Ocean to keep Aquitar in control of the major trade routes. Ral Doré is often called a pirate by Eastern nations but his a hero in Aquitar.

Common Missions/Plot Threads

Silent Running - With the loss of large sections of mainland Eutheria, Aquitar's colonies are where their power lies now. Keeping control of these areas is up to the navy and more importantly, the Bleu Septembre. You never know when the ship will be sent into a dangerous area, outnumbered and their only advantage is stealth.

Dig Too Deep - Undermining Inc has Under-Housing projects in nearly a dozen cities now but was mammal truly meant to dig so far beneath the earth? Who knows what some poor excavator may find while clearing a new tunnel. Will the workers be able to stop a horrible exomorph incursion AND stay on schedule and under budget for their construction?

Testing Science - You never know what new project you'll be assigned when you go to work at Undermining Inc, or worse, if you'll be assigned to test a prototype. Don't just cross your fingers and hope the ground crew knows what they're doing. You'll have to keep the project from failing and make sure it is a financial success.

THE CIVITAN TRADE ALLIANCE

Recent History

After increasing paranoia came to a head following the Aqui-Civitas War, many of the independent city-states along the Mare-Civitas, the main body of water along the southern edge of Eutheria, went into extreme isolation, out of fear of absorption into bigger nations. Several of the remaining, open nations set about through subterfuge to reunite the city-states. Beginning as a number of smaller trade agreements, these were eventually joined together through clauses buried deep in their contracts. The resulting Civitan Trade Alliance is still relatively unstable, with the numerous Doges or Dukes of the city-states never able to agree on anything but they are at least trading again.

People of the Nation

Capybara

Indigenous to the southern areas of the continent of Vespuccia, Capybara were the first people to meet the colonizing Civitans. At that time they were nearly extinct, hunted and enslaved by the Jaguero, the dominant empire of southern Vespuccia. Since that time the Capybara have allied with the Civitans and fought back against their oppressors. While most remain in and around New Muriccio, some have emigrated to other city-states, often working as merchant marines, protecting trade vessels, to make their way.

Chipmunks

Native to the city of Venture and recently of the fortress at Ste. Ermina. Chipmunks have been the foremost smiths and weapons designers on the Mare-Civitas for centuries. Their work has been so lucrative that they are capable of maintaining their own Mercenary Company to defend their city, rather than simply renting soldiers to protect them. This advantage makes them one of the more dominant species in the Trade Alliance.

City Mice

The most numerous species in the Trade Alliance, city mice can be found nearly anywhere. They range all the levels of society but are generally seen as lower class, working menial jobs, or as ill-equipped mercenaries. City Mice are also usually uncomfortable outside of cities, unable to effectively defend themselves against raiding bandits, or attacking armies. City Mice build their towns in easily defensible or escapable locations.

Jumping Mice

Before the foundation of the Rodentian Empire's capital, Muriccio, on the southern coast, Jumping Mice were the only indigenous people of the island of Brisica. Jumping Mice are mountain and forest dwellers, living in the high altitude city of Zapus. These mice are excellent athletes and hold a yearly competition to show their prowess against international competitors.

Sardan Pikas

Jungles are the home of Sardan Pikas, particularly the jungle island of Sardus, furthest Civitan island from the mainland. Pikas are excellent hunters and trackers, having lived closer to nature than most of their allies. Pikas often find work as guides or bounty hunters, preferring to stay on the trail. More amoral Pikas also find work as hired killers or military snipers.

The Leaping Lancers
Military, Mercenary

In the ancient days of Brisica, before the Rodentian Empire founded its new capital on it, Zapus was the sole city on the island. For centuries, Zapus' claim to fame was the Leaping Lancer competitions. An athletics and acrobatics competition with a focus on martial arts, Leaping Lancers drew in competitors as far away as Vandalands and Khonshu. After the foundation of Muriccio on the coast of the island, Zapus formed a militia of loyal participants to keep the city free from Rodentian rule. Keeping the name Leaping Lancers, the new militia kept Zapus independent and eventually developed into a full mercenary group. Due to the restrictive recruiting policies, the Leaping Lancers is a very small mercenary company.

Key Facets of the Leaping Lancers
Juan Chamomile, Lead Lancer

Still a mouseling when the Hyperian War began, Juan made a name for himself after being the youngest winner of the Leaping Lancer competition. Over the ten years of the Hyperian War, he rose through the ranks and made a name for himself in bars and beds across the Mare-Civitas. After Armando Reyas, the previous commander, lost his life in the Battle of Helios at the close of the war, Juan was elected the new Lead Lancer.

The Hyperian War and Zapusian Independence

During the outset of the Hyperian War, the Leaping Lancers fought on the side of their long time allies, the Civitan City-States. Due to a number of legal contracts of the mercenary company, Zapus was effectively a member of the coalition. Though the war had drawn on too long and both sides were becoming involved in other wars, the rivalry between Hyperia and Civitas brought both to the brink of destruction. If not for the actions of Reyas and Chamomile, the nations would have destroyed each other and left scraps for the invaders. Since the close of the war, the Leaping Lancers have kept Zapus independent from Civitan politics and the city out of the Trade Alliance. Leaping Lancers have idealized their mercenary work, selecting jobs based on their own morality and the effect on civilian populations.

Zapusian Lance

A light yet sturdy hybrid of the mounted lance and a throwing spear, the Zapusian Lance was designed to be aerodynamic increasing the terminal velocity of a jumper. Though it was designed centuries ago at the inception of the Leaping Lancer competitions, the Zapusians are sure its design is as effective as they claim.

Leaping Lancer Competitions

A martial arts competition that brings in competitors from around the world. It is held yearly in Zapus, bringing in an amazing revenue to the tiny city and a fresh crop of candidates for the mercenary company. Winners, in addition to collecting a cash prize and a Zapusian Lance, are invited to become members of the Leaping Lancers. Scouts in the crowd may also select other competitors who have potential.

Organizational Structure

Leaping Lancers work in small units called bands. While superiors set basic policy for all Leaping Lancers, each Lancer can take his own mercenary contracts and after showing enough skill, can build their own bands. Part of displaying the ability to run your own band is taking one or two athletes training for the competition under your wing and helping them develop their skills.

White Roses

An affectation of Juan's time in Hyperia that became popular with all lancers, the white rose is left by modern lancers on the battlefield and in the bedroom. The flower represents justice and purity to the Leaping Lancers and a sign of their committal to a mercenary contract but the opposite to the lady of the house. Soldiers and husbands dread finding a white rose, forever keeping their eyes to the sky after discovering one.

Ranks

Competitor (Recruit)

Requirements - Grow up in the city of Zapus and train as a lancer your entire life, or compete in the yearly athletics competition. Anyone who enters may call themselves a 'Leaping Lancer'.

Lancer (Private)

Requirements - Winning the Leaping Lancer competition, or performing well enough to be scouted allows entrance into the mercenary company. Getting past the preliminaries requires showing Acrobatics and Athletics skills of at least 30%. Dedicate at least 1 POW to the Leaping Lancers.

Rewards - A Zapusian Lance to all Privates and a cash prize of 100 gold to the winner of the competition.

Compulsions - A Leaping Lancer should always put fame and the adoration of crowds, before getting paid. 10% of all mercenary contract pay must be sent on to the Commander.

Trainer (Sergeant)

Requirements - Raise Acrobatics, Athletics, 1H Spear or 1H Spear & Shield Combat Style and at least 2 other organizational skills to 50%. Dedicate 3 POW.

Rewards - Two Lancer trainees (Underlings) who you help develop into full Leaping Lancers.

Compulsions - Your trainees are not your personal bodyguards, treat them as students, not soldiers. Put enough time into developing their skills so that they can eventually rise through the ranks like you. 10% of all mercenary contract pay must be sent on to the Commander.

Band Leader (Officer)

Requirements - Seduce at least one noble's daughter or wife, following in the path of Juan Chamomile. If seduction is not your forte, find another way to win the hearts of the lower class (buying a lot of rounds at the local tavern is a good start). Dedicate at least 8 POW.

Rewards - When determining your influence among nations and any organization, combine your POW and Leaping Lancer Dedicated POW for any appropriate skill scores. Your Trainees are no longer available, as they have gone off to compete; but you can no begin recruiting your own micro-band of Leaping Lancers. Lancers work in small groups of 5-10.

Compulsions - Take care of your fledgling band, take missions and contracts of high moral standing. Leaping Lancers represent the best of the best. Stand tall and never sully the name. 10% of all mercenary contract pay must be sent on to the Commander.

Lead Lancer (Commander)

Requirements - While there is currently no room at the top, when a vacancy comes up each band leader casts a vote for a new commander. The Commander must have his own band and have won the Leaping Lancer competition at least once (rather than simply have been scouted).

Rewards - The Targe MkII, this Hyperian designed shield is the mark of the Commander in the Leaping Lancers. 10% of all Leaping Lancer income comes to the Commander to maintain their facilities and the city of Zapus. The Targe MkII is a Hoplite Shield that may be used to attack as a free CA during Striking Leap and gains all the bonuses.

Compulsions - A bit of hero worship occurs amongst lancers and their commander, they will follow you and mimic your quirks and habits but the ideal of the heroic and just mercenary must still be upheld. Additionally, each year the Commander must preside over the competition and present the winner with his winnings (from the Commander's own pocket).

Organizational Skills
Athletics, Evade, Influence, Acrobatics, Seduction, Streetwise, Survival, 1H Spear & Shield Combat Style, 1H Spear Combat Style

Current Divisions and Commanders
Band of the White Rose and Zapus High Command - The Band of the White Rose is the current ruling band of Lancers and maintains Zapus High Command, the tower fortress in the mountainside of Brisica. The Band is famous across the world for its expertise in battle and in swaying the people they fight for.

Juan Chamomile of Brisica, The White Rose - Juan is a charismatic Jumping Mouse, who has always shown passion for his ideals and for women of war-torn Eutheria. This habit has placed him on the enemies list of many nobles and monarchs. His love affair with Tetra, the daughter of the Tyrant of Hyperia shocked many Eutherians.

Band of the Flying Partizan - A multi-species Band, the Flying Partizan takes on underdog contracts, seeking to help revolutions in infancy, or protecting small villages from bandits.

Ludwig von Jeney - The gerbil commander of the Flying Partizan, Jeney once fought as part of the Dishonor Guard against the Knights Bubonic, seeking to return their lands to the rule of the Kaiser of the Vandals. While mostly unsuccessful, when the Dishonor Guard was folded into the State Army, Ludwig took his ideals with him to the Leaping Lancers, winning the athletics competition against more famous athletes and eventually founding his own mercenary band.

Common Missions/Plot Threads
Mercenary Contracts - Many requests come to the Leaping Lancers but is each contract appropriate for the Lancers? Judging each contract by its moral caliber is important to remaining a Leaping Lancer.

Prison Break - Lancers have a penchant for getting into trouble with city guards, or cuckolded nobles. Getting fellow Lancers out of prison is a common task for trainees. Just don't kill anyone that doesn't deserve it.

SONS OF SARDUS
Military, Mercenary

A mercenari group that is known for its fierce fighting style and expertise in scouting, tracking and jungle warfare. Hailing from the jungle island of Sardus, Sardan Trackers work independently and usually take contracts to hunt criminals or to find missing persons. Some are even hired as navigators or guides for their pathfinding skill. It is not uncommon to find Sardans attached to Civitan Marine squads during combat in unfamiliar terrain, or even hired by foreign militaries fighting abroad.

Key Facets of Sons of Sardus
Emmanuel Sardus

Descendant of Prolagus Sardus, Emmanuel is fresh to his work as Head Tracker. The disappearance of his brother Enrique, only a few years ago, still weighs heavily upon him. Their father, Victor Sardus, had still been Head Tracker and the brothers had rarely taken contracts. The two decided to divide up a series of contracts and in a quirk of fate, his brother went to Vespuccia while Emmanuel went to Khonshu. Emmanuel devotes a large portion of his time to investigating his brother's disappearance and similar cases, swearing to ensure better safety to his mercenaries.

Origin of the Sons of Sardus

The heads of the organization trace their lineage back to Prolagus Sardus, the Rodentian hunter who tracked down and rescued Emperor Flavius' son from Hyperian bandits. As reward for his service, Prolagus was gifted an island on the far edge of the Rodentian Empire. The jungle island was uninhabited and, supposedly, the creatures that lived there were horrible monsters. Sardus spent a number of years exploring the island and hunting the creatures that lived there. Eventually he settled along the northern coast, founding a small port town that would become Sardus City. The Sons of Sardus were originally the hunters that protected farmers and merchants as they explored the island seeking out the indigenous crops for export. Eventually their skill was learned of in the outside world and they formed an actual organization to represent them and get work.

Individual Mercenaries

As more feet on the ground make it harder to follow tracks, Sardan Trackers work alone or, at most, in pairs. This arrangement provides a large monetary gain from completing contracts but Trackers, while expert hunters, are no elite warriors. They are never hired as bodyguards or infantry. The Sons of Sardus only come together to vote or discuss policy. In such meetings each Sardan Tracker has equal say: one knife, one vote. For the duration of a meeting they take up residence in a bar or other local establishment and vote by stabbing their knives into the tables. You can easily pick out a tracker hangout by the pockmarks in the tables.

Condottieri Accords

Forced into law by Doge Felix Doria of Sardus, the Condottieri Accords are named after his son. Condottieri Doria was killed during the occupation of Sardus City by Civitan mercenaries working for the Aquitarans. The Condottieri Accords are required by all mercenaries seeking employment in the Trade Alliance. By signing the Condottieri Accords, a mercenary agrees to only fight for The Civitan Trade Alliance or her current allies. A mercenary agrees never to attack civilians, except in self defense. A mercenary agrees to commit no other crimes under the laws of the nation they fight for, under increased penalty of death or life imprisonment. The actions of any contract signer are held accountable by their fellow signers, if the mercenary is dead before convicted, or if their fellow signers cover for the criminal activities, actively or by omission. As many Sardans were abused or killed during the occupation of Sardus City, the mercenaries of the island take the Accords very seriously.

Skills outside of Mercenary Work

When not fighting in wars, the Sardan Trackers find employment in exploration and pathfinding, or working as bounty hunters. The majority of the Sons of Sardus' income actually comes from this non-military work.

Rank

Citizen (Recruit)

Requirements: While most Sons of Sardus are Sardan Pikas, other species that have emigrated to the island also call themselves Sardans and are free to join the mercenary group.

Scout(Private)

Requirements: Any 4 Organizational Skills at 30%, Must be a citizen of Sardus and sign the Condottieri Accords. Dedicate 1 POW

Rewards: A Sardan Knife, a blade somewhere between a machete and a skinning tool, is the iconic weapon and symbol of a Son of Sardus. It counts as a Shortsword with the Anatomical Precision Tactical passive applied to it (despite being a medium weapon and having no medical training). You may also take mercenary contracts through a Sardan intermediary. As a scout, you may only take scouting or exploration contracts, no Scouts may be signed on for the purposes of fighting.

Compulsions: Every Sardan mercenary must follow the Accords, no group takes the rules written down in it more seriously. Even if the law does not string you up for violating it, the Sardans will. To take mercenary contracts through a Sons of Sardus intermediary, a mercenary must show their Sardan Knife as proof of membership.

Hunter (Sergeant)

Requirements: Any 4 Organizational Skills at 50%. Complete at least 5 Scouting contracts. This allows you to take a bounty contract through an intermediary. Completing your first bounty promotes you to the rank of Hunter. Dedicate 4 POW.

Rewards: A compass is presented to Hunters, as they have shown their skill of trekking the world with only their guile. The compass in addition to determining cardinal directions, provides +10% to Track or Survival for pathfinding and navigation. You may now take bounty hunting contracts and other combat oriented contracts, expanding your selection. An increase in the danger pay you receive is given from such contracts.

Compulsions: Hunters have the same compulsions as Scouts, additionally, they are expected to appear at meetings at least once a year, usually the first day of June.

Tracker (Officer)

Requirements: Any 8 Organizational Skills at 75%. Complete at least 5 Bounty contracts. This allows you to take an extraction contract through an intermediary. Completing your first extraction contract promotes you to the rank of Tracker. Dedicate 8 POW

Rewards: Camouflage fabric is gifted to trackers to craft stealthy clothing. Clothing made out of camouflage fabric provides +20% Stealth. You may now take rescue and extraction missions. While most nations allow bounty hunters to cross their borders to seek out criminals, mercenaries seeking to rescue kidnapping victims or extract spies caught behind enemy lines are less likely to be allowed across borders. For this reason such contracts are available only to highly trained Sons of Sardus.

Compulsions: Trackers have the same compulsions as Hunters, additionally it is the task of Trackers to hunt down violators of the Condottieri Accords for the Trade Alliance. A number of Trackers are often simply 'on call' for this sort of work and paid a stipend of 25 Gold Murin a month for not taking any other mercenary work. A 100 Gold Murin reward is given for the successful live capture of violators.

Head Tracker (Commander)

Requirements: The Head Tracker is re-elected each year at the height of summer on the first day of June. Unless events have been extremely unfavorable, the Head Tracker runs uncontested and receives little or no 'nay' votes. When a new Head Tracker is required, the mercenaries of the Tracker rank nominate candidates and then they are voted on immediately.

Rewards: Sons of Sardus are very easy going when around each other, as the Head Tracker you find it easy to get others to do things for you, add your influence critical range to Duty rolls for political favors even if you don't have the Cult of Personality Tactical Passive. If you do have the passive, receive double your influence critical range, or add your influence critical range to the bonus from seduction or courtesy.

Compulsions: The Head Tracker is a representative of the Sons of Sardus and has the voting power of a Doge in the Trade Alliance, despite having no city-state to rule. In addition to acting on behalf of the Sardan Trackers in this political manner, it is also the duty of the Head Tracker to solve internal disputes and cast tie breaking votes in internal meetings (otherwise the Head Tracker does not vote, merely presiding over meetings).

Organizational Skills
Survival, Streetwise, First Aid, Track, Athletics, Insight, Perception, Lore (Any Ecological Biome), Any Small or Medium Size Combat Style

Current Divisions and Commanders
Sardus City - The closest thing the Sons of Sardus have to a headquarters are the local establishments of Sardus City. Any meetings held as a group simply select a bar or eatery and occupy it for a few hours while discussing their issues and grievances.

Emmanuel Sardus - Part union leader, part spokesman, the Head Tracker ensures contracted mercenaries are paid well and follow the Condottieri Accords. It is also the Head Tracker's responsibility to settle disputes between trackers. Emmanuel has no real power over other Sons of Sardus though, he cannot give them orders or deny them work.

Common Missions/Plot Threads
Discovery - Sardan pathfinding lends itself well to acting as a guide to scholars hoping to discover a lost city, or a new species. Sons of Sardus may not be able to fend of armies of soldiers but they can keep such contractors safe from eating the wrong plants or walking off a cliff.

According to Sardus - Hunting down a familiar face is a horrible task but the Condottieri Accords are the highest law for mercenaries. Sardans know this all too well and if your target is another Son of Sardus, your work will be cut out for you.

Venture Company
Mercenary, Exclusive Technology

One of the early proponents of the Mercenari military system in the Civitan City-States, Venture Company is a mercenary group from the city of the same name. For many years Venture Company was similar to any other mercenary groups but as firearms became prominent in Eutherian warfare, Venture's more learned citizens became skilled in firearms design and manufacture. This influx of quality firearms resulted in Venture becoming the forerunners of most weapons technology and their mercenaries became equipped with top of the line weapons.

Key Facets of Venture Company
Doge Tamias

The current Doge, or Duke, of the city and company of Venture, Tamias has become an expert in a number of fields. Acting as one of the three lead members of the Trade Alliance, Tamias has worked heavily in his autumn years, traveling back and forth across the Lemurian Ocean to keep the foundling government in one piece. He has had little time of late to work on his passion, weapons design.

Fort Ste Ermina

Originally a City-Fortress of the Knights Fusilier, an order of knights who used captured Scyzantine firearms in the 2nd Crusade, Fort Ste. Ermina was captured by Venture Company after bandits attacked the city of Venture from the stronghold. Since 1775, the Venturans have held the city against any assault, even against armies that far outnumber the defenders.

Panzardi Speciale

The successful defense of both Venture and Ste. Ermina is due to the weapons developed by Venturan engineers. A focus on heavy weapons and siege weapon alternatives has lead to their most famous design, the Panzardi Speciale, a wheel mounted machine gun. Easily Operated by two people, the Panzardi Speciale can put out more ammunition than an entire squad of soldiers with regular firearms of the era.

Marine Assault Vehicle

Also known as a MAV, the Marine Assault Vehicle is a small steamship designed for amphibious deployment of soldiers, able to traverse seas and land, the MAV is a recent development of the Venturans in a joint project with Federwerk. The MAV solves a number of issues for the sea-based nation, allowing troops to assault island-based targets without needing to use docks, or rowboats to land.

Joint Federwerk-Venture Projects

During the Aqui-Civitas War, Doge Tamias saw a chance to cement an alliance with Federwerk Industries, a Vandal weapons development firm. These two companies began designing joint projects, using technologies from both groups to create better weapons. This political arrangement has led to Venture Company further testing the waters of the political landscape and arranging other alliances, including being key in the foundation of the Trade Alliance.

Ranks
Independent Mercenary (Recruit)

Requirements: Mercenaries from other companies often find employment in specialized capacities in Venture Company. As Venture knows its strength and weakness, they will augment their forces with other specialists, such as hiring Sons of Sardus as scouts or Leaping Lancers as storm-troops. For some, this is a foot in the door for the most successful mercenary group.

Mechanic (Private)

Requirements: Showing a Mechanisms, Craft(Firearms or Artillery) and Engineering skill of 30% is the minimum requirements to be hired by Venture Company. Dedicate 1 POW to the Company upon hire.

Rewards: Mechanics receive 1 Gold Murin monthly along with room and board in Venture or Fort Ste. Ermina.

Compulsions: Mechanics manufacture and repair the weapons of Venturan Mercenari. These employees keep the guns firing. Mechanics are not true mercenaries and are not allowed to take contracts or fight, except in defense of the city or fort.

Engineer (Sergeant)

Requirements: Raising your Mechanisms, Engineering, Craft (Firearms or Artillery) and Drive Skill to 50% and dedicating 4 POW allows a Mechanic to receive a promotion to Engineer.

Rewards: Engineers handle the daily operations of Fort Ste Ermina and Venture city-state, receiving 5 Gold Murin monthly. Additionally, Engineers can sign up as limited Mercenaries to operate MAVs in battle.

Compulsions: Mishandling of daily operations can see a demotion for an Engineer or expulsion from Venturan lands. As limited mercenaries, Engineers are not allowed to operate weapons and receive only 20% of the contract fees (taken from the Mercenari's 90%).

Venturan Mercenari (Officer)

Requirements: A 75% skill in Mechanisms, Firearms or Artillery Combat Style and Commerce shows an Engineer is ready to become a Mercenari and fight for Venture. Dedicating 8 POW and signing the Condottieri Accords, for the restricted behaviors of a mercenary, allows promotion to this rank.

Rewards: Venturans operate in teams of two and if you did not have a Squad Mate from Exemplarism, you are matched up with another Mercenari as your Squad Mate. Additionally a Panzardi Speciale or Venturan Mortar is provided for your use when fulfilling contracts assigned to you by the Doge. In small situations only one or two weapon teams may be sent to fulfill a contract but in times of war dozens of squads will be assigned to a contract. You and your Squad Mate split 90% of the contract's fees for your own use and to pay for the repairs to your equipment. The last 10% is given to the Company itself to manage upkeep of its holdings.

Compulsions: Following the Condottieri Accords is important to Venture, this newly formed agreement in the Trade Alliance has been signed by most minor mercenary companies, as well as the Sons of Sardus and Venture Company (The Leaping Lancers are a rebellious holdout). By signing the Condottieri Accords, a mercenary agrees to only fight for The Civitan Trade Alliance or her current allies. A mercenary agrees never to attack civilians except in self-defense. A mercenary agrees to commit no other crimes under the laws of the nation they fight for, under increased penalty of death or life imprisonment. The actions of any contract signer are held accountable by their fellow signers if the mercenary is dead before convicted, or if their fellow signers cover for the criminal activities, active or by omission.

Doge of Venture (Commander)

Requirements: Tamias has entered his autumn years and has gone on his last mission. He is currently seeking a successor to take over after he leaves this world. He has a number of Mercenari in mind but none have yet to make a legitimate case. The Doge is looking for someone not only of high engineering and mechanical skill but a born diplomat who has loyalty to the company, that will not run the group into the ground after he is gone.

Rewards: The Doge is the ruler of both the city of Venture, the Fort at Ste. Ermina and a mercenary company. While the monetary flow alone makes such a commander a powerful person, the control of weapon designs, several thousand mercenaries and two cities makes the Doge one of the three most powerful leaders in the Civitan Trade Alliance, alongside the Governor of New Muriccio and the Doge of Muriccio.

Compulsions: The political webs that exist between the city states must be carefully managed, the young government of the Trade Alliance could collapse due to any mismanagement by its charismatic leaders.

Organizational Skills

Craft (Firearms or Artillery), Mechanisms, Engineering, Commerce, Combat Style (Firearms or Artillery), Drive

Current Divisions and Commanders

Fort Ste. Ermina, Civitas - The primary stronghold of the Venturan mercenaries, this fortress was attacked almost a dozen times during the Aqui-Civitas War and the besiegers were repelled each time. With the open terrain surrounding the fortress, the Venturan guns were able to zero in on key sections of enemy forces from nearly a mile away. Combined with a well kept farm within the castle walls, the fort is nearly siege proof.

Capitaine Rufus - A newly promoted chipmunk, Rufus was born in Fort Ste Ermina but left early to join a mercenary group. After spending half a dozen years abroad, he returned home to join Venture Company and quickly rose through the ranks.

Venture, Civitas - Nestled in a river valley not far from the coast, Venture has relied on mercenaries to defend its vulnerable position for years. But with the quarries and mines throughout the valley, Venture has fortified the area, setting up weapon teams in key positions along the hillsides to keep the passage into the city defensible.

Doge Tamias - An aging veteran, Tamias has fought in hundreds of battles. As his time on the battlefield has come to an end, he has retired to his home town and left younger chipmunks to make war.

Common Missions/Plot Threads

Marine Assault - With the majority of Civitas being small islands, many battles occur on them that require MAVs. Picking the right assault point can be as key to success as anything that happens after landing. MAVs are partially armored but not enough to survive direct cannon fire.

Soldier of Fortune - The Condottieri Accords can tie a mercenaries hands but the consequences are severe. If your fellow mercenaries are breaking the rules, as a contract signer you are responsible for their actions unless you bring them to justice. Do you reveal their injustice or cover for your brothers in arms?

Weapons of War - The weapon designers of Venture Company are always coming up with something new and sometimes its the new mechanic's job to test it out. Lucky for you the death rate for weapon testers is only 1 in 4, those are good odds!

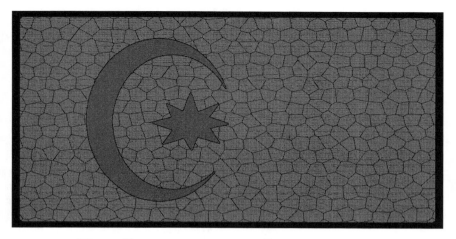

THE SULTANATE OF SCYZANTIUM

Recent History

At the turn of the century, the Sultanate sought to expand the territories of the nation. Seeking to obtain a port with access to the Lemurian Ocean, the Vizier found an Ally for the campaign in Aquitar. His correspondence to the Emperor never revealed the failing mind of the ruler and an alliance was struck, sparking the Aqui-Civitas War and the Hyper-Scyzantine Wars. Although Aquitar was nearly destroyed, the Vizier deployed assassins to disrupt Aquitar's opponents. The military power of Civitas thus distracted, Hyperia became Scyzantium's only opponent to taking the coastal territory. The effective political maneuvering of the Vizier and the adept military tactics of the Sultan, elevated Scyzantium to a true power in Eutheria. With the coastal territories in the Mare-Civitas and control of the Principality of Khonshu, Scyzantium now controls the primary trade routes to the far east.

People of the Nation

Agamids

Once the dynastic Sultans, after their overthrow by the Varanid Dynasty, the Agamids became nomadic healers and scholars. The current Vizier can track his lineage back to the Agamid Dynasty but shows little urge to regain his power. Agamids are still scholarly today, working better as the power behind the throne, whether that be for the Sultan, or for merchant lords, or criminal syndicates. Agamids never seek to step into the spotlight again.

Anoles

The Fortress Island of Adwaita is home both to the Anoles and their beasts of war, the Siege Tortoises. These massive creatures have long been the manner through which the small Anoles have remained independent but after a disastrous siege of the city, the Anoles

133

acquiesced to supplying the Sultan with their siege weapons. Anoles continue today as weapons designers. Those with less inclination to such work are often spies, or other dubious occupations, using their small size to their advantage, able to get into places many of the larger reptilians cannot.

Chameleon

Before the arrival of Scyzas and the thousands of escaped slaves that followed him over the decades after his 'rebellion', the chameleons were the dominant species of the deserts. They are still quite numerous but their predisposition to remaining hidden keeps census takers from determining the actual population. This expertise in stealth remains with them today and helps them find employment as assassins or scouts. Rare Chameleons have stepped away from the deserts to become merchants or travel the world but deep in the southern deserts is the most likely places to find them.

Desert Monitor

The nomadic Varanids travel in a massive circle through the desert, returning to the north every few centuries. During one such pass, they ousted the Agamid Dynasty and became the ruling Sultans of Scyzantium. While a rare few continue their nomadic path, most have become nobles or upper class merchants, ruling cities across the country. Varanids can be quite anachronistic, preferring the ancient ways of their people but, due to being thrust into the spot light, struggle to balance their new duties with their wandering ways.

Gecko

Exiles from the eastern land of Bharat, the Geckos are a recent addition to the population. They brought with them their small riding turtles which are faster and easier to handle than the Anoles' tortoises. Gecko long rifles were also introduced to the Scyzantines at that time and Geckos fulfill a cavalry role in the military. Outside of war, Geckos are excellent guides and trail markers, most having ridden across the desert many times over.

Sand Lizards

Depending on the total population of Chameleons, Sand Lizards are the first or second most populous species in the Sultanate. As the tales of the Hero Lizard spread across the Rodentian Empire, many escaping slaves set their eyes upon the desert, following him out of the reach of the mammals. They quickly became the work force of Scyzas and the backbone of the Sultan's armies. Their continued worship of Scyzas as a hero and savior has kept the Sand Lizards loyal to the Sultanate even though the current Sultan is of a different dynasty.

THE ASSASSIN'S GUILD
Mercenary, Exclusive Religion

One of the oldest contiguous organizations in the world, the Assassin's Guild began their underground resistance against the Rodentian Republic around 100 BF. Since the foundation of the Scyzantine Sultanate, the Assassin's Guild has found a home in the Scyzantine Quarter of Lacerta, a border town between Aquitar and Scyzantium on the shores of Lake Tiberias. Its agents are experts in espionage and assassination, with the bulk of their number being chameleons, the world's natural stealth fighters.

Key Facets of the Assassin's Guild
Hassan Kusuuf

The title of the commander of the Assassins and the name of a commander from the 8th century AF. After dying in combat against a Rodentian General, Hassan's second in command impersonated him during his later, successful, assassination of General Pyctoris. The rumored immortality of Hassan Kusuuf spread amongst the Assassins' enemies and lead to his name becoming the title of the leader. Each commander who takes up the mantle has their name scrubbed from the Guild's records and their deeds added to those listed for Hassan Kusuuf.

Assassination

The Assassins are the original killers for hire but unlike common hit men, the assassins follow a code of conduct that does not allow them to kill without a contract. When hired in times of war, their contracts are often left with blank areas to include the names of those they kill, or a list counting numbers of slain. This practice never sits well with the Assassins, who prefer to eliminate as few targets as possible to perform their goals but their debt to the Sultanate stresses their ideals at times.

Loyalty to the Sultanate

Over the centuries since Scyzas stumbled out of the desert, favors have been passed both ways but when the modern Varanid Sultanate took power, they sheltered the Assassins from their opponents, including the Eutherian Knightly Orders and ensured their survival. This debt to the Sultanate has seen to the priority of any contracts that bear the Sultan's seal and a flexibility in their usual policy.

Lacerta

Since the founding of the Sultanate, Lacerta has been the headquarters of the Assassins. While the city has changed hands many times over the centuries, at least a small cell of assassins has always operated within the city. Today, half the city is owned by Aquitar and the other half by Scyzantium. In the Scyzantine Quarter, the tunnel works that lead through the Bayawak mountains to Agaminople are controlled by the Assassins.

Organizational Structure

With Hassan Kusuuf as the commander, the Imams determine what contracts each Assassin will receive and train neophytes in their basic skills. Beneath the actual assassins, the neophytes are torn down from their core beliefs until any point of morality or ethics could be seen from any angle in their minds, until any event could be seen as simple fact. 'Nothing is Forbidden, Everything is Permitted'.

Religious Iconography

'Nothing is Forbidden, Everything is Permitted' - The mantra of the Assassins, it represents their view of the world, partly a comment on morality but also on the futility of the actions of any one person. Poetically, they attempt to do as little as possible to make the largest changes, killing a single person or retrieving a small piece of information to change the world.

Ormaz and Ahriman - The Assassins are followers of a branch of Zarath, the ancient faith of the desert before the rise of the Scyzas Hero Cult. Unlike other followers of Zarath that see the balance between good (Ormaz) and evil (Ahriman) as a battle of will, Assassins see it as a true battle, their elimination of evil being the path to saving the world. This has put them at odds with the few orthodox Zarathi who see their actions as fuel for Ahriman.

Ranks

Recruit

Requirements - The only public location for the Assassins is in the city of Lacerta. Any citizen of Scyzantium can present themselves there for indoctrination and follow the basic religious beliefs of the Assassins, which are available for any reptiles.

Neophyte (Private)

Requirements - Possessing Stealth, Disguise and any Combat style of at least 50% may catch the eye of an Imam who will seek to perform full indoctrination of a recruit, taking a year to fully train them into a true assassin. Dedicate at least 3 POW.

Rewards - Access to an indoctrination site, where the Neophyte will learn about the world from the Assassin's view and train to kill with precision and stealth.

Compulsions - Neophytes are not permitted to leave the site of their indoctrination until the year long course is completed. Leaving before this training is complete will bring down the fury of the Imams, whose duty it is to slay rogue Neophytes.

Assassin (Sergeant)

Requirements - Training your Stealth, Disguise, Combat Style and 2 other organizational skills to 75% and the completion of Neophyte indoctrination. Dedicate at least 5 POW.

Rewards - A full member of the guild, Assassins may take contracts selected for them by the Imams; Guild contracts pay exceedingly well. Unlike Neophytes, Assassins are free to return to their lives, have access to Assassin hideouts throughout the world and may succeed in political favors automatically while on a guild contract. Such automatically succeeded favors take their cost from the final fees paid to the Assassin.

Compulsions - Your identity as an Assassin, the location of Guild properties, or any other secrets of the guild must be kept hidden from the world. Failure to safeguard the actions of the Assassins will bring down the fury of the Imams, whose duty it is to slay rogue Assassins.

Imam (Officer)

Requirements - Twelve is a holy number to Assassins and as such, the leaders of the guild always total 12, including the Hassan. When a position is open amongst the Imams, an Assassin is selected by the other Imams and groomed for the position. Coming into favor of a majority of the Imams is an effective way to guarantee your promotion to this rank. Dedicate at least 8 POW.

Rewards - You assist in the training of neophytes and selecting contracts for assassins to undertake. 25% of all contract fees is split amongst the 11 Imams.

Compulsions - You must never betray the secrets of the guild, additionally, it is the duty of the Imams to hunt rogue Assassins or Neophytes. If Imams betray the guild, it is solely the duty of Hassan to hunt them.

Hassan Kusuuf (Commander)

Requirements - Each Hassan selects one of the Imams as his second in command, if the Hassan should die in battle without naming an heir, his second is automatically raised to commander. If the Hassan's wounds are grievous but leave time for him to name an heir, he may select one of the other Imams but his opinion rarely changes after selecting his second in command.

Rewards - The absolution of your previous life, whoever you were before is gone, you are now Hassan Kusuuf, a 1200 year old assassin that has killed thousands in his life time. Command of the Assassins is yours.

Compulsions - Your old life is gone, If you attempt to leave your life as Hassan, the assassins will remove any loose ends; friends and family; and end your life as well.

Organizational Skills

Athletics, Evade, Insight, Perception, Persistence, Sleight, Stealth, Acrobatics, Disguise, Streetwise, Survival, Track

Current Divisions and Commanders

Scyzantine Quarter, Lacerta - The Reptilian half of the international city of Lacerta is home to numerous Assassin hideouts, the exact locations are a secret of the order and the headquarters cycles randomly to keep the leaders safe. Some of these hideouts are also linked into the underground tunnels that cross the deserts, allowing the Assassins to travel out of sight.

Hassan Kusuuf - A chameleon has held the name/title of Hassan Kusuuf since the original. As their old life is stricken from the records, the original identity of the current leader is unknown.

Common Missions/Plot Threads

Spy Contracts - Some clients may only want information, or details on the whereabouts of their enemies. Theft is not a speciality of Assassins but stealing missives, or other strategic artifacts may fall within a Spy Contract.

Assassin Contracts - An assassin is always prepared to stain their blade. Any target is viable but Assassins will refuse all but the sultan if they must slay innocents, or kill indiscriminately to access their target. Precision is key to the Assassin's philosophy.

Religious Mantra - Assassins count for the largest population of the shrinking Zarathi faith. As such, they often perform missionary work, or pilgrimages to the holy places of Ormaz. The unique philosophy and culture of their religion also entices those that have lost their faith in other religions and many new recruits are introduced to the guild through this missionary work.

Fortress Adwaita
Mercenary, Exclusive Technology

An ancient island fortress, Adwaita has been the habitat of massive tortoises and miniscule Anoles for more than a millenia. These two species have lived symbiotically, working together to defend their tiny island nation. In the last few centuries they joined the outside world, allying with the Scyzantines and have since set to operating the siege weapons of the Sultan, mounting them to the shells of the walking behemoths, as the tiny lizards operate the cannons.

Key Facets of Fortress Adwaita
Choris al-Iguan and Seychelle

The dual chiefs of Fortress Adwaita, each representing their species, work together to run the island. Choris al-Iguan is a relatively young Anole, being paired with Seychelle, the tortoise, after the death of his father, Eque al-Iguan III. Before taking his position, Choris and Seychelle took a journey to see the outside world and, upon their return, set in place a number of reforms.

Tortoise and Anole Symbiosis

Anoles and Tortoises have worked symbiotically for centuries. As Anole Nobles come of age, they are paired with Tortoises who act both as mentors and guardians. The Tortoises inability to use tools is compensated by the Anoles working the fields to grow crops and building weapons, armor and structures. The tortoises act as war platforms and scholars. Living upwards of three hundred years, they are able to accrue vast amounts of knowledge and share it with their Anole compatriots.

Siege Weapons

As gunpowder came over the Bayawak Mountains from Chugoku and firearms supplanted bows and ballisatae, the Anoles built foundries to cast large cannons known as 'Efrits'. Designed with the strength of tortoises in mind, Efrit cannons were mounted to the shells creating mobile artillery. This setup allowed the Adwaitans to defend their islands from the Scyzantines and Marluk Geckos for generations, able to quickly move their artillery across the island to any location under assault.

Allegiance to the Sultan

Eventually the sieges and particularly rough storms ruined the crops farmed on Adwaita and unable to access food from the mainland, the Adwaitans were forced to surrender to the will of the Sultan. The

Sultan agreed to maintain food supplies for the Tortoises if they would swear allegiance to Scyzantium and answer the call to defend the nation. Choris' ancestor, Eque I and a young Seychelle agreed to this arrangement and the Siege Tortoises have since become an asset to Scyzantine warfare.

Riding Turtles

During their journey, Choris and Seychelle lived with the Geckos and their turtle steeds and formed an alliance with them. Adwaita would begin designing weapons appropriately sized for the smaller turtles and the Geckos would let the Adwaitans share their land, providing more territory for the tortoises to train and live.

Great Dermochelys

A gift, after the Punitive Expeditions to Khonshu, from the newly formed Principality, the 'Great Dermochelys' is a giant sea turtle, larger than many naval vessels. Dermochelys has been placed under the control of Fortress Adwaita who strapped a dozen turret cannons to her shell, providing a Flagship for the Scyzantine Navy. Believed to be an ancient Bahamutian, Dermochelys is a sapient creature but speaks too deep and slowly for most creatures to comprehend. Tortoises of Adwaita are able to translate for Dermochelys relaying her words to Scyzantines.

Rank

Citizen (Recruit)

Requirements: Living on Adwaita, or along the nearby coastlines of the Geckos, any civilian has a connection to the Fortress, the Tortoises often journey through the towns, either out for training or simply to see the sights.

Metallurgist (Private)

Requirements: Craft (Metalsmithing, Firearms, or Artillery) 50%, Gecko or Anole Species and Dedicate 1 POW.

Rewards: New workers are always needed to cast Cannons or other siege weapons. A weekly stipend of 2 Gold Solidus for working the forges.

Compulsions: Work is weekly and no long term commitments are required, except keeping details of the layout of Fortress Adwaita, or information about any operations from rival weapons manufacturers. While working the forges, you cannot leave Adwaita until a week's work is complete.

Rider (Sergeant)

Requirements: Drive and Ride 75%, Heroic Command 50% and Dedicate 4 POW

Rewards: A Riding Turtle if you already have a Squad Mate through Exemplarism, or a Siege Tortoise as your Squad Mate. A monthly stipend of 5 Gold Solidus and their Turtle or Tortoise will have its medical and food needs met by any Sand Guard supply post for free.

Compulsions: Riders of Adwaita must heed the Sultan's call when war threatens the nation. If this pact is broken, the Rider is stricken from the records of Riders able to have their supply needs met by the Sultan and their monthly stipend is lost. If paired with a Siege Tortoise, the rider should remember they are sapient, can communicate and are not simply items to be owned. They should not simply be treated like a steed.

Siege Rider (Officer)

Requirements: Engineering and Mechanisms 75%, Heroic Command 75%, Dedicate 8 POW

Rewards: Your Siege Tortoise is mounted with a Cannon, Howdah, or other Siege Machine. If a Turtle rider, you are placed in charge of a squad of riders, who you command in battles the Sultan calls upon you for. Your stipend is raised to 10 Gold Solidus and a parcel of land on the coast near Adwaita is given to you and your Tortoise to split.

Compulsions: Same compulsions as a Rider.

Chieftains (Commander)

Requirements: Commerce, Influence and all previous skills 80%. Dedicate all POW. If Seychelle dies, as could happen with his advanced age, A new set of chieftains is selected, even if Choris is still alive. Such a selection is determined by the Siege Riders.

Rewards: You and your Tortoise companion are made the dual Chieftains of Fortress Adwaita. The sultan provides a stipend of 1000 Gold Solidus for the operation of the island, from which your personal stipend is taken (likely 100 Gold Solidus) depending on the quality of your rule.

Compulsions: It is the duty of the Chieftains to run the island fortress wisely, as their rule can be revoked by three quarters of the Siege Riders voting against them. As your Tortoise companion has shared control of the city, you must come to agreements and compromises if you have clashing personalities.

Organizational Skills

Drive, Ride, Engineering, Commerce, Mechanisms, Craft (Metalsmith), Craft (Firearms), Heroic Command, Combat Style (Artillery)

Current Divisions and Commanders

Fortress Adwaita, Scyzantium - The island nation is known by this name because of its 10 meter cliffs running around nearly the entire island, making it difficult in the best situations for a naval assault. Nearly the entire island is cultivated for crops, with Tortoises spending the majority of their time in the waters around the island and the Anoles building their homes in the rough areas too sparse to farm.

Choris al-Iguan and Seychelle - The Dual Anole and Tortoise chieftains of Fortress Adwaita, they manage the island and all their territories along the eastern coast. Fresh to siege warfare, Choris has brought a number of clever ideas, particularly the armoring of Tortoises for use as rams and rapid loading cannon shells.

Aqabad, Scyzantium - Nestled in a cove along the southern coast of the Bharatese Ocean, Aqabad is home to the largest Gecko population in Scyzantium, when they migrated into the deserts from the Bharatese city of Marluk, they brought thousands of riding turtles with them. These semi-aquatic steeds were a perfect addition to the once small port of Aqabad, now a bustling center of trade and the Scyzantine Navy.

Kelsey Manji - The Gecko representative for Adwaita operates from Aqabad, getting jobs for Riders in the navy or as small transports along the coast. Manji is also the 'captain' of Dermocheyls, commanding the crew that operates the guns mounted to her shell, letting the great sea turtle direct herself in combat.

Common Missions/Plot Threads

The Turtle Mariner - The aquatic nature of Turtles and Tortoises lends to their use as natural ships. A large portion of the trading vessels of the Bharatese Ocean are alive. Such work can prove dangerous though, as a Cannon does much more permanent damage to a living creature compared to a repairable ship.

Bring Down the Walls - Cannons are the siege weapon of choice in modern times, their strength in numbers can destroy cities or castles. Even a single Tortoise can take out a bandit camp or sway the outcome of a skirmish. Of course, being on the receiving end of Mobile Artillery can be a horrific experience!

THE HERO CULT OF SCYZAS
Exclusive Religion

The major religion of Scyzantium is focused around Scyzas, the reptile that first successfully rebelled against the Rodentian Empire and went on to found the Sultanate. His likeness adorns thousands of statues, mosaics and paintings and each is worshiped by his followers. This Hero Cult extends to his 'descendants' and the reigning Sultan is seen as a spiritual successor to Scyzas, by some worshippers. The founders of the Hero Cult were Sand Lizard refugees, escaping slavery from the Rodentian Empire. While other species may take up the faith, Sand Lizards continue to make up the majority of the followers.

Key Facets of the Hero Cult of Scyzas
Conflict with Zarath

As the religion bloomed with the rise of the Sultanate, it came into conflict with the established religion of the desert, Zarath. Sultans following Scyzas attempted to subjugate the Zarathi, forcing them to convert to the Hero Cult. These minor wars forced most of the Zarathi to go into hiding and camouflage their cities to keep outsiders from discovering them. Though in modern times, with the large majority of Scyzantines being Hero Cultists, Zarathi are able to come out of hiding without worry of persecution, they are still isolated culturally.

Dynastic Change

The primary schism between the two cults of Scyzas differ on whether Scyzas' species, or sultanate is the more important key to his worship. When the Varanid Dynasty ousted the Agamid Dynasty from its rule of the Sultanate, the two schools of thought became divided over the new Sultan's divinity.

Religious Iconography

Scyzas - The hero of all reptiles, Scyzas escaped from slavery in the Rodentian Empire, causing a cascade that led to the foundation of Scyzantium and the collapse of the Rodentian Empire. During his reign as Sultan, Scyzas did little to quell the religion, focused on keeping his foundling nation from being destroyed. As a result, the faith expanded from simple idolism to direct worship.

'Tell my tale to those who ask. Tell it truly, the ill deeds along with the good and let me be judged accordingly. The rest is silence.'

Lacerta - The Wife of Scyzas, Lacerta was slain during their escape, dying on the shores of Lake Tiberias. The early capital of Lacerta was founded on the site in her honor. She is seen as a symbol of sacrifice to create divinity and the duty of all Hero Cultists to give up their lives for Scyzantium.

Pyctoris - The Slaver and Rodentian General who owned and tracked Scyzas into the desert. He was eventually slain by Chameleon Assassins. Praetor Pyctoris is depicted as a demonic figure and embodies all the evils Eutherians have wrought upon the world.

Path of Scyzas - A ritual pilgrimage that takes disciples from their homes out to the Danidan river in Eutheria, where Scyzas' tribe once lived. They must then travel into Muriccio in 'search' of Lacerta. Finally they must travel back to the Danidan River and follow it to the shores of Lake Tiberias, before spilling a small portion of their blood on the shores, in honor of Lacerta's death. While in the time of the Crusades this was a feat of heroism, with the uneasy peace, the Civitans are just happy for the trade and tourism.

Rank
Observer (Recruit)
Requirement: Being raised on the culture and lore of the Hero Cult, or adopting the holidays and practices of the Hero Cult while remaining neutral in faith, many Scyzantines are simply observant of the religion.

Adherent (Private)
Requirement: Learn the basic of the life of Scyzas by gaining Lore (Hero Cult) 30% along with 4 other Organizational skills at 30%. Dedicate 1 POW.
Rewards: Your own copy of the Book of Scyzas, All organizational skills have +5% as long as you carry this book and remain a member of the Hero Cult.
Compulsions: Study the Book of Scyzas, it should never leave your side.

Hafiz(Sergeant)
Requirement: Gain Lore (Hero Cult) 100% and transcribe a copy of the Book of Scyzas and gift it to a new Adherent.
Rewards: If you have Faith I, your Book of Scyzas provides +10% to all organizational skills. A Hafiz can also make a modest living off the transcribing of the Book of Scyzas or any written works.
Compulsions: A Hafiz must share his knowledge with others, any who ask of Scyzas should be shared of his tale.

Faris (Officer)
Requirements: Any Melee Combat Style 50% and 4 Organizational Skills 80%. Dedicate 8 POW.
Rewards: A Scyzantine Scimitar is forged for the Faris, the knights of Scyzas. This Weapon has the basic profile of a Scimitar but benefits from Faith II and the Book of Scyzas as if your Combat Style were an organizational skill.

Compulsions: A Faris must travel the Path of Scyzas once every five years, to show their dedication to the Hero Cult. Their normal duties consist of protecting their Caliph and in times of war, supplementing the Scyzantine Army. Many Faris act as commanders in the army or navy.

Caliph (Commander)

Requirements: Background: Urban (Upper Class), Profession: Noble. Dedicate all POW

Rewards: The Faris of the Hero Cult swear fealty to the Caliph and they are his to command. Each denomination of the Hero Cult has a different number of Faris, resulting in either a small gang, or a powerful army.

Compulsions: The Caliph is part warlord, part religious leader, with the sprawling desert between Agaminople and the dozen or so Caliphates, the Caliphs rule their cities almost independently. Put just as the Faris swear fealty to the Caliph, the Caliphs swear fealty to the Sultan and they are at his command.

Organizational Skills

Oratory, Lore(Hero Cult), Culture(Scyzantium), Survival, Persistence, Teaching, First Aid, Healing, Art

Current Divisions and Commanders

Cult of the Sultanate - Agaminople, Scyzantium - The current capital of Scyzantium is also the headquarters of this variant of the Hero Cult. The Cult of the Sultanate believes that the spirit of Scyzas lies in the Sultan, regardless of what Dynasty is on the throne.

Salah ad-Din Varanus ibn Suley - The oldest son of Varanus and the Caliph of the Cult of the Sultanate.

Varanus ibn Suley - The object of worship by Sultan Cultists, Varanus has grown to a venerable age and is rarely seen in public, letting his son perform ceremonies.

Cult of Agamids - Iguabul, Scyzantium - Based in the old capital, originally called Agaminople, The Agamid Cultists believe that the spirit of Scyzas lives in his descendants, who are scattered across the desert. Agamids are generally not a part of this cult but from time-to-time an Agamid may get delusions of grandeur and believe themselves to be the incarnation of Scyzas.

Exigua al-Gilis - A Sand Lizard who's ancestors fought for the Agamid Dynasty. When the Varanids deposed the Agamids, the al-Gilis family followed them into the desert, continuing to worship the true spirit of Scyzas. The Agamid that the al-Gilis followed named their family Caliph upon his death, for their sworn duty. When the capital moved from Iguabul, previously known as Agaminople, Exigua moved his Caliphate to the abandoned city and slowly returned it to its former glory.

Common Missions/Plot Threads

Path of Scyas - Faris and other 'adventure' seekers travel the Path of Scyas, reliving his life in fast forward, imagining all the slavery and hardship, while traveling around Eutheria. This used to be a real adventure, with angry Herpetiphobes in every village. Now many of the war weary cities are grateful for the income the mass of pilgrims provide.

ZARATH
Exclusive Religion

The oldest religion of the desert, centers around the war between the gods Ormaz and Ahriman. It has mostly been supplanted by the Scyzas Hero Cult but is still followed in small pockets far from Agaminople. Zarath is most common among Chameleons and Monitors, the original denizens of the desert before the arrival of the Agamids, Geckos and Sand Lizards. Due to the Varanid Dynasty coming from a Zarathi background, the religion has seen a growth in popularity among the newer populous of the desert but is still far behind the Hero Cult of Scyzas.

Key Facets of Zarath

Ormaz

The creator, Ormaz has warred with Ahriman since before life walked the earth. This war was once simply fought in the spirit world but as djinn broke through the barrier into the world created by Ormaz, life began to bloom and their war was brought to the material realm. The lives of each person are filled with deeds, words and emotions and each good action or intent helps Ormaz in his battle. With this in mind, Zarathi attempt to lead good lives, always seeking to protect the creations of Ormaz.

Ahriman

The destroyer, Ahriman feeds upon evil deeds, words and emotions, winning his war with each horrible death and wicked act. While Zarathi avoid such events, they do not avoid life. Living life is itself a creative act, empowering Ormaz over Ahriman. As the souls of the living were sent to the material world to accrue good deeds, avoiding life defeats the purpose of their existence. Zarathi do not defeat Ahriman by avoiding sin and excess, they revel in the glories of life and the creations of Ormaz.

Urvan

The Old Reptilian word for Soul, an Urvan is a person who travels to experience life. Their goal is to fill their lives with good actions and experiences, when they die, their soul will return to Ormaz and empower him. Along with Faravahars, Urvans created the nomadic culture prevalent in the deserts before the founding of Scyzantium.

Differences with the Assassins

A number of differences separate Orthodox Zarathi from the Assassins of the northern deserts.

The monastic structure of the Assassins and its exclusionary setup is against the concept of Zarath which seeks to share the knowledge of Ormaz's war with all, to recruit 'soldiers' in their spiritual war.

The Assassins' militaristic activities, choosing to eliminate those they see as 'followers of Ahriman', is only empowering Ahriman. Zarathi see good in all souls and believe that allowing 'evil people' to live they may attone in the future and perform good deeds to balance out their evil actions.

Assassins see hell as a place of punishment and torture, the domain of Ahriman, rather than a place of reformation, where souls with evil are cleansed. This form of eternal damnation is against the Orthodox Zarathi view.

Ancient Cities of the Desert

A number of 'lost' cities of the Zarathi exist in the southern deserts, founded by the Monitors before their nomadic ways. It is rumored some of these cities still exist, with Zarathi villagers still living there, near the cradle of sapient life. One of the most famous of these lost cities is Avestan. Legends say the city was built into canyon walls with gigantic statues of Ormaz and Ahriman clashing across the chasm. Only a few of the Zarathi nomads know if these rumors are true but they have yet to give up these locations to outsiders.

The Six Yazatas

Old Reptilian for 'Worthy of Veneration', these are the six religious leaders of Zarath. Structured off of the 6 'elements' of the material world, each Yazata works to protect a portion of Ormaz's creation. Zarathi believe in a non-structured society and the Yazatas act more as scholars or wise-men rather than religious authority. The only Zarathi they have command over are the Faravahar, who have sworn to protect them.

Faravahar

The guardians of ancient Reptilia, Faravahar are holy defenders, bodyguards of the Yazatas and nomadic warriors who seek to right wrongs and injustices. Their's is a difficult path, never seeking to kill or do evil themselves on their journeys. These nomadic adventures are only undertaken by a few Faravahar at a time, most of their life is spent near the Yazatas, protecting them and the future of their religion.

Conversion

The uninitiated who believe in the existence of Ormaz are known as Kushad, or 'naked', seeing the world for what it is but unprotected from evil deeds. Zarathi believe in 'uncovering' others, relating their beliefs in the world but never seek to convert Kushad to Behdin, or followers. The initiation of a Behdin requires a great deal of introspection and study of religious practices. Eventually an initiate performs a ceremony, tying and untying the Kushti, a cloth belt representing their faith protecting them from evil deeds. A Zarathi must replicate this ceremony each day, tying and untying the belt 7 times, once for each Yazata and finally for Ormaz. The ceremony ends when the belt is tied the 7th time.

Ranks

Kushad (Recruit)

Requirements: Having the basic beliefs of Zarath shared with you is enough to be a Kushad, beyond this point the choice to convert and complete the Behdin ceremony is your own choice.

Behdin (Private)

Requirements: Lore(Zarath) and Culture (Zarath) 30%, dedicate 1 POW and complete the Behdin ceremony.

Rewards: a Kushti belt, provides an additional point of Armor to the abdomen if you have taken the Faith I Tactical Ability.

Compulsions: Performing the prayers and belt tying ceremony everyday is a necessary part of protecting oneself from Ahriman. Performing evil deeds is also un-Zarathi and could result in exile, as Zarathi do not wish to surround themselves with evil.

Urvan (Sergeant)

Requirements: Survival 50%, Track 50% and dedicate 4 POW.

Rewards: A sudreh, or undershirt is gifted to Urvan to protect them on their journey. This provides an additional point of armor to the chest if you have taken the Faith II Tactical Ability.

Compulsions: In addition to the prayers and kushti ceremony, an Urvan must devote his life to a pilgrimage to anywhere and everywhere. Urvan only return to their home to become Faravahar.

Faravahar (Officer)

Requirements: First Aid 75% , Healing 75% and any melee Combat Style 75% and dedicate 8 POW.

Rewards: A melee weapon of your choice is forged and blessed by the Yazatas. Zealous Strike can be used as a defensive Combat Maneuver, allowing you to strike back against your foes if you successfully parry with this weapon.

Compulsions: Faravahar defend the Yazata from those who would seek them harm. From time to time, a Faravahar is sent on a pilgrimage like an Urvan but must seek out injustice and right it. This is a difficult task as a Faravahar must never attack first, only fighting in defense.

Yazata (Commander)

Requirements: Oratory, Lore (Zarath), Culture (Zarath) and 2 other Organizational skills at 90% and dedicate all POW. There are, at any one time, 6 Yazata and the death of one results in a year long mourning period, before the other 5 Yazata select a Faravahar to raise up.

Rewards: Five Faravahar act as your bodyguards and will lay down their lives to save you. These are not mere Squad Mates or underlings, the Faravahar should have normal Hit Locations and health.

Compulsions: It is the duty of the Yazata to share, learn and transcribe the scriptures of the Zarathi faith. Additionally, each Yazata devotes their life to the betterment of a particular element of the world.

Organizational Skills

Oratory, Healing, First Aid, Lore (Zarath), Culture (Zarath), Survival, Track, Language (Zarathi)

Current Divisions and Commanders

Agaminople, Scyzantium - Modern Zarathi flock to the city of Agaminople as one of the iconic members of the faith, the Varanid Sultan Varanus IX, reigns from the city. While a large number of Zarathi now live there, coming from a nomadic culture, Zarath is spread across the entire country.

Yazata Thustra - The Yazata of Bahman, the element of beasts and all living creatures. It is the duty of the Monitor Lizard Thustra to improve the lives of all sentient creatures.

Yazata Ya Fulan - The Yazata of Ardwahist, the element of light and fire. It is the duty of the Chameleon Ya Fulan to share knowledge, whether it be the knowledge the Zarathi faith, or modern science.

Yazata Tuhitar - The Yazata of Sahrewar, the element of metal and minerals. It is the duty of the Tortoise Tuhitar to study the stars and determine the destiny of the universe and all creation.

Avestan, Scyzantium - One of the famous lost cities of the Zarathi, Avestan hides in the southern desert, a place only Faravahar, the Yazata and the denizens of the city know the location of. Faravahar and Urvan are the only people to leave the city.

Yazata Bihman - The Yazata of Spandarmad, the element of the earth. It is the duty of the Monitor Lizard Bihman to act as caretaker of the Zarathi cities, maintaining their splendor and keeping their locations secret from outsiders.

Yazata Kudam - The Yazata of Xurdad, the element of water. It is the duty of the Chameleon Kudam to heal the deserts of their arid plight. Once the deserts were lush and green but the watertable beneath the land ran dry and the Xurdad Yazata have sought ever since to right this evil.

Yazata Aghyar - The Yazata of Amurdad, the element of plants. It is the duty of the Mongoose Aghyar to ensure the growth of plants and crops in the Zarathi cities and share food with the needy. Aghyar is not Aquitaran but a native of Khonshu and born Zarathi.

Common Missions/Plot Threads

Pilgrimage to Nowhere - Urvan and Faravahar journey the world with no particular goal, this can go on for their entire lives, or they may find some event or realization that calls them back home.

Difficult Choices - Zarathi have specific guidelines for their lives and letting evil roam is a necessary restriction upon them. Expediting evil back to Ahriman is no solution to the ills of the world.

Death of Daevas - The only true evil in the world are the Daevas, known as exomorphs to outsiders, Daevas live beneath the desert and stalk the world. Zarathi see no compulsion in sparing Daevas from sending them back to their master. The Ancient cities of the Zarathi sometimes come under attack from these creatures and the Faravahar rise to the occasion to save the cities.

The Vandalands

Recent History

The rise and fall of the Knightly Orders of the crusades has crippled the Vandalands. Once the nation was unified under the Vandal Kaisers but has been cut up by the Knightly Orders, who ruled each of their territories autonomously. As the Knights dissolved, each Graf or Count went back to ruling their own county and only acted unified in times of war. A number of dissenters have sought to return Kaiser Hedgehauser to a true place of power and weakening the influence of the last Knightly Order, the Knights Bubonic. This dream of a single true Vandal nation has yet to come to fruition but if it does not come soon, the crusades will either bankrupt the entire country or invite a war that breaks their armies.

People of the Nation

Gerbils

From the county of Federwerk, the Gerbils represent the best minds of the Vandals but their combat prowess leaves much to be desired. Until the invention of their clockwork armors, Gerbils were treated more as tinkers, making interesting baubles or novelties. Now Gerbils stride into battle alongside seasoned veterans, standing face-to-face with the great Ursal Bears and Wolves of the northeast.

Hamsters

Roving bands of hamsters came out of the north in the ancient days, to smite the Rodentian Empire and then they went home for a drink. Hamsters are famous for their ravaging and their revelry. They are civilized enough to make boats, armors and weapons but the harsh winters and beasts of the northern fjords are too difficult to form a real civilization. Instead those that roam south latch onto the culture of the Vandals and are nearly tolerated by their neighbors.

Hedgehogs

Ermindorf, the capital city and county of the Vandals is home to the largest Hedgehog population, including the Kaiser of the Vandals. While making up little of the nobility, Hedgehogs are mostly of the lower class and make up a large portion of the King's Own Hussars. The only noble hedgehog is the Kaiser and only because of adoption into nobility far back in his lineage. Hedgehogs are generally hardworking and callous people, while the neighboring Aquitarans revolted over a single corrupt king, the Vandals ignored the near collapse of their entire nation.

Shrews

As in Aquitar, nobles of the Vandalands are commonly Shrews. Unlike in Aquitar their nobility is still a mark of respect and Shrews live comfortable lives, except when war threatens, when they cast their lives down like any soldier for their kaiser. A popular pastime for Shrews of the river-lands is avianism; riding, breeding and training kiwi birds for cavalry.

Vandal Rats

When the threat from the south rose and the Knightly Orders began to form during the crusades, Rats were the first to join and fight the reptilian menace. In the centuries in between, their vision of honorable knights, gallantly defending faith and freedom, has died. Rats make up a large portion of the criminal element, including the political extremist group, the Dishonor Guard. Some still remain members of the Knights Bubonic but such members are often of the highest echelons, fanatical in their devotion to the cause.

Federwerk Industries
Mercenary, Exclusive Technology

The City of Federwerk has long been the most famous border town in the Vandalands. Abutting onto territory with the Ursal Khanate, populated by wolves and bears, the people of Federwerk would never have stood a chance against border skirmishes if not for their engineering expertise. Introduced to the world in the 1300s, the mechanical marvels known as Valkyr were originally wood constructs, armor suits that augmented the strength of the gerbil engineers who built them. They would call themselves the Valkyr Corp. Since their original deployment, repelling an army of wolves at the city gates, dozens of redesigns have been made but eventually the Valkyr Corp became outdated and few working models continued to be used in war. When Count Gotz von Federwerk lost his arm during a battle in one of the antique designs while fighting under the banner of a Knightly Order, Gotz returned to Federwerk and set to redesigning the Valkyr. The new designs he created were built of metal and far more sturdy. Reform the old Valkyr Corp, Federwerk Industries is now a major power in Vandalands, able to build an army with educational training instead of physical prowess.

Key Facets of Federwerk Industries
Count Gotz von Federwerk

Before losing his arm, Gotz was a crass young mercenary who fought in battles across the Vandalands, mainly against the Ursal Khanate. After having his arm severed by a bear's jaws, Gotz became a focused engineer, no longer a wastrel but a force of science and politics.

Valkyr Corp. and the Knightly Orders

The mishandling of the Vandalands army under the Knightly Orders became a key point of Gotz's efforts on the political stage. Though all but the Knights Bubonic have since collapsed into obscurity, the Valkyr Corp are still not the primary soldiers of the Vandal army. Gotz has been able to steer the Vandalands away from its self-destructive crusades in recent years but the Corp is still merely a mercenary company.

Joint Federwerk-Venture Projects

While Gotz attempt to press for a people's army, over a knight's army, he has turned to Venture Company's weapon designs and managed to create a number of joint projects between the two city-states. While these projects are still in development, the technologies developed so far have made Federwerk the most powerful county in the Vandalands.

Organizational Structure

Beneath Count Gotz, are each of the Viscounts controlling the territories of the county. Independent of the Nobility are the Engineers that make up the actual Industries of Federwerk. Some devote their skills to developing Valkyr designs while others work in Venture to marry the Civitan weapon designs to Valkyr suits.

Ranks

Citizen (Recruit)

Requirements - To become a member of Federwerk Industries, one must move to the county and become a citizen. As the county is the company, living and working there makes one an employee.

Assistant/Private

Requirements - To actually work in the industrial complexes, a citizen must display Mechanisms and Engineering skill of 30%.

Rewards - Placement in either Design or Valkyr Corp. Assistants in the Design department make 25 Thaler each month and Privates in the Valkyr Corp make 50 Thaler a month.

Compulsions - Federwerk is a business, competency matters over political opinion or actions outside of work.

Designer/Sergeant

Requirements - In Design, an Assistant must show Mechanisms, Engineering and at least 1 other skill at 50% and have presented an effective design to their superiors. Valkyr Sergeants must get Mechanisms, Engineering and a Combat Style to 50%

Rewards - A monthly stipend for Designers of 50 Thaler and 100 Thaler for each effective design submitted. Sergeants receive a 100 Thaler stipend and their own Valkyr.

Compulsions - Poor design work, or a lack of submitted designs might see the demotion of a Designer. Sergeants must train Privates in Valkyr operation and join their fellow sergeants in completing mercenary contracts.

Lead Designer/Officer

Requirements - Promotion to Lead Designer requires Mechanisms, Engineering and two other organizational skills at 80%. Valkyr Officers must increase their Mechanisms, Engineering and Combat Style to 75%.

Rewards - A personal workshop and increased stipend of 200 Thaler, with a continual 100 Thaler for designs submitted for Lead Designers. Valkyr Officers receive new, top of the line Valkyr MkIIs and 3-4 of sergeants under their command and a stipend of 200 Thaler.

Compulsions - Designers must continue to submit designs for approval but can also oversee the approval of other designs and the construction of such projects. Officers in the Valkyr

Corp command a small squad and select mercenary contracts for them to undertake. 10% of any contract fees are the Officer's to keep, while the rest is returned to Federwerk for the upkeep of the Valkyr.

Count (Commander)

Requirements - The position of Count is hereditary and Gotz cannot have children after a disastrous clock winding accident. There is no heir apparent but it is expected one of the Viscounts will succeed him. Though a particularly charismatic officer or designer could win his good graces and find themselves into his will. Dedicate at least 10 POW to get the chance to win over the Count.

Reward - Control of the most powerful county in the Vandalands and its major industrial complexes. Additionally, Gotz's personal Valkyr, an older model but equipped with a flame cannon of his own design.

Compulsions - Loyalty to the crown of the Vandals and the just rule of the territory granted to you.

Organizational Skills

Perception, Commerce, Craft, Engineering, Mechanisms

Current Divisions and Commanders

Grafschaft von Federwerk (County of Federwerk) - Federwerk Industries is the County of Federwerk, a mountainous region in southeast Vandalands. As the Knightly Orders collapsed, Federwerk took possession of many of their abandoned castles, expanding the overall size of the county. The county has nearly complete autonomy but Gotz seeks to reunite the numerous semi-independent states under the Kaiser of the Vandals.

Count Gotz von Federwerk - The noble mercenary, Gotz fought in a number of battles in his 30 year career. As a gerbil in Valkyr armor, Gotz often had an advantage over his opponents and believed that creation and invention was a superior tool to victory over numbers, or strategic trickery.

Common Missions/Plot Threads

Repair Duty - Valkyr are worth more than their pilots, after a battle every working piece is recovered and any scraps are turned into something better.

Launching! - The Valkyr Corp is a mercenary group that has a number of contracts with the Vandal Army but also some small groups. A Valkyr Pilot never knows where he'll be sent next.

Exchange Student - With the joint projects between Venture and Federwerk, a Valkyr engineer may get sent to work in Civitas with engineers there on weapon or armor designs.

Weapon Test - Designs result in prototypes that have never been used before. Cross your fingers and hope you don't explode in front of your superiors.

THE SKYGUARD
Mercenary, Exclusive Technology

After the redevelopment of Valkyr by Federwerk Inc., the Kaiser pressed for development of additional designs to give the Vandalands a technological edge in war. While most of Federwerk saw redesigns of the Valkyr as the future of weapons design. Ferdinand von Starkvind, recently retired to the clockwork city, saw the skies as the key to war superiority. After a number of arguments with designers, the city was split between Valkyr and Airship ideals. Ferdinand took a number of agreeable scientists with him to the nearby mountain town of Steinausderram. There he and his colleagues set to designing and building the world's first airship. While their first prototype crashed in 1812, by 1815, the *Starkvind I* was completed and successfully flown. When the airship was shown to Kaiser Hedgehauser he instated Ferdinand as Brigadier General von Starkvind and placed an entire battalion at his command to train. The Skyguard became an independent group of Air Privateers in 1818 operating from their mountain hold. By 1820 a second functional airship was completed, the *Starkvind II*, along with a reconciliation with Federwerk, allowing them access to the rocket technology designed for Valkyr Mk IIs. This allowed the Skyguard to raid other vessels without landing the airships, by sending their troops rocketing aboard.

Key Facets of The Skyguard
Brigadier General Ferdinand von Starkvind, 'The Skylord'

A veteran of domestic and foreign wars, Starkvind was the original pioneer of airships. He is the current commander of The Skyguard and Captain of the *Starkvind I*. Getting on in age, he has generally left command to his immediate subordinates and the Captain of the *Starkvind II*, Otto von Wiegraf. During the period between his retirement from the military and his settling in Federwerk, Ferdinand claims to have traveled the mountains of the Vandalands and visited the lost Avian Roosts. It was this adventure that lead him to believe flight was the next big development in warfare.

Captain Otto von Wiegraf

Originally a young member of Federwerk's design staff, Otto joined Ferdinand's airship venture in 1812 after the crash of the *Steinausderram*, the prototype ship. With his assistance, the *Starkvind I* lifted off in three years, half the time of the original design. His dedication to the Skyguard has continued into his promotion to Captain and he currently commands the *Starkvind II*.

Stein aus der Ram
Named after the town, the prototype airship and the subsequent crash, Stein aus der Ram (Stone of the Ram), is a Vandal musical sextet performing music in the 'New Vandal Hardness' sub-genre. The group has become famous around the world and performed from Ermindorf to Jackson, DV. The Skyguard itself is disappointed by their choice of name, with nearly a hundred scientists and engineers killed in the crash of the *Steinausderram* and despite the band requesting performing for the Skyguard (preferably aboard an airship), they have, to date, been denied.

The Starkvind I and Starkvind II
The first operational airships of the Skyguard, the *Starkvind I* was completed in 1815 and the *Starkvind II* in 1818. Armed with cannons and marines like a naval vessel, the airships can hold nearly 20 knots. With no wars yet to face the Skyguard, they have acted as Privateers, raiding foreign ships along the coast, patrolling for bandits, and protecting the borders of the Vandalands. Newer, smaller ships are currently on the assembly line and the *Starkvind I* and *Starkvind II* will be the flagships of the northern and southern battle groups, respectively. Until that time the Two ships usually work in tandem to perform their tasks.

Organizational Structure
With Starkvind followed by Wiegraf at the top of the hierarchy, a number of squads of Sky Marines operate aboard each flagship equipped with Federwerk 'Assault Assistance Packs'. Each ship also has a crew of 200+ engineers and gunners. On the ground, the base crew at Steinausderram numbers in the thousands. Although structured like a military, the Skyguard is an independent organization with its own rules and is able to hire domestic or foreign workers.

Ranks
Recruit/Employee (Recruit)
The Skyguard requires a minimum of 2 year military service with any nation before being eligible as a recruit and further promotion. Employees are any workers who's skills are used to keep the base at Steinausderram running and help in the construction of new airships.

Marine/Mechanic (Private)
Requirements - Minimum 2 Year military service in any national army or navy. Those with at least 50% Engineering skill are put on the Mechanic track, trained to repair and pilot the airship and operate its weapons. Soldiers, with a focus on combat skills, are made members of the Sky Marines.

Rewards - Sky Marines are trained in firearms use if they have not already been trained and equipped with an Assault Assistance Pack (AAP). Mechanics are trained in the operation of an airship and its weapons, additionally they gain +10% Heroic Command and are placed in a station of the ship (Guns, Engine, Security, Helm). Each rank provides +5% to the skill related to their station (Guns - Combat Style Artillery, Engine - Mechanisms, Security - Combat Style Firearms, Helm - Drive). Like the military, a Stipend of 100 Thaler is provided during active duty.

Compulsions - Crews of airships are on two month cycles, receiving a month off-duty after each cycle. AWOL soldiers will find it difficult to outrun an airship. If crewmen are consistently tardy for their cycle, they may be stricken from the records and marked as a deserter in both the Skyguard AND Vandal armies.

Sergeant/Chief (Sergeant)

Requirements - Served at least 6 cycle with the Skyguard, Sky Marines must have raised their Mechanism skill to 50%, showing competence with an AAP. Mechanics must raise their skill to 80% and have served for at least 10 cycles.

Rewards - Sky Marine Sergeants are issued Repeater Carbines, a better weapon for use while equipped with an AAP, or in the midst of enemy troops. Chiefs and Sergeants gain a crew of 2-3 mechanics/marines below them in their station of the airship. During active duty a 200 Thaler stipend is provided and during off-duty months a 100 Thaler stipend is provided.

Compulsions - Sergeants and Chiefs are expected to manage their crews nearly autonomously. Service continues in two month cycles.

Officer/Master Chief (Officer)

Requirements - Served a total of 18 cycles with the Skyguard, successfully managed your underlings without abuse of rank, excess endangerment, or mutiny (or at least reports thereof).

Rewards - Command of the entire compliment of Sky Marines aboard an airship for an Officer. The Master Chief is now a member of the bridge crew and often directly in command of the ship during a shift. Both ranks now provide a stipend of 400 Thaler per month during active duty and 200 Thaler during off-duty cycles.

Compulsions - Responsibility aboard the airship is expanded to either all the Sky Marines, or all the Mechanics. Any actions or crimes taken by those under your command are on your head.

Captain (Commander)

Requirements - Converted to a 4 month on, 1 month off duty schedule. The completion of a new airship other than the *Starkvind I* or *Starkvind II* (or an empty Captain's seat on either ship). Only those on the Mechanic track can be promoted to Captain, Officer is the maximum rank for a Sky Marine. A Heroic Command of 50% and an Engineering of 100% is also required.

Rewards - Command of your own airship, the repair, maintenance and operation is all yours! Your stipends are increased to 800 and 400 Thaler.

Compulsions - Each airship is placed in either the Northern or Southern battlegroup and given a portion of the nation to patrol. Every two months a cycle changes up and the ship is brought back to refuel, repair and switch out crew. While general autonomy is provided to each ship or battlegroup (as the fleet expands, some ships will be partnered up), not returning to base for a cycle change, or forcing your subordinates to perform actions against their standing orders results in Heroic Command conflicts and repercussions with the Vandals.

Organization Skills

Athletics, Acrobatics, Engineering, Mechanisms, Shiphandling, Heroic Command

Current Commanders

Starkvind I - The first functioning airship off the Steinausderram production line. It has seen service for over five years and has been replaced by the *Starkvind II* as the primary flagship but is still the pride and joy of Ferdinand von Starkvind, its creator.

Brigadier General Ferdinand von Starkvind, the Skylord - Always considered a quirky rat, Ferdinand appears mad to many outsiders but his passion for his work on airships has resulted in the entire field of aerial warfare. Growing elderly, Ferdinand von Starkvind leaves much of the daily operation of the Skyguard to Wiegraf and the dozen or so Officers of the Sky Marines.

Starkvind II - A superior vessel to the *Starkvind I* due to the integration of new weapons developments from the joint projects between Federwerk and Venture.

Captain Otto von Wiegraf - Originally a young gerbil on Federwerk's design staff, Otto joined Ferdinand's airship venture in 1812 after the crash of the *Steinausderram*. With his assistance, the *Starkvind I* lifted off in three years, half the time of the original design. His dedication to the Skyguard has continued into his promotion to Captain and he currently commands the *Starkvind II*.

'Now witness the firepower of this fully armed and operational airship!'

Common Missions/Plot Threads

Bandit Patrol - Bandits are a continual problem across the Vandalands, the vast and varied terrain make it difficult for ground troops to attack their outposts and castles. The Skyguard is often brought in to eliminate particularly exacerbated threats.

War Games - On occasion it is necessary to test the skills and weapon systems of the Skyguard, as such, mock battles are held annually in the skies above Ermindorf. These competitions between the crews draw many spectators from across the nation to watch the battle from the ground below.

Open Skies - The utility of airships is not lost upon the Vandals and some expeditions are planned for the near future, to do trade with far away nations that would otherwise be out of reach of the small Vandal navy. These expeditions seek to go boldly where no rat has gone before.

The Cult of Wodin
Exclusive Religion

Wodinism is the principle religion of the northern hamster tribes. Modern records consist of a loose collection of stories of ancient gods who were lead by Wodin, the All-Hamster. In many of these stories, there are tales of slaying trolls and ettin, multi-limbed beasts with rock-like skin.

Wodin was the key figure in many tales, a hamster of great size, who's left eye glowed golden and bright. Wodin's eye was stolen by Lokke, the Wolf trickster god, who would replace his own eye with it and raced around the world to become the sun. Each night it would be returned by the flying shadows, who would replace it with Lokke's original silver eye.

After generations of fighting evil and ordering the chaos of the world, Wodin travelled into the east, to guide the hamsters of the far lands. He promised his followers in the west that he would return one day to lead them again.

Key facets of Cult of Wodin
Arctos Nevsky, Wodin Reborn

Modern followers of Wodin believe that his promise has come true in the body of Arctos Nevsky, the Prince of Novagrad. An Ursal bear who lost his left eye in combat against Vandal Crusaders. After his defeat at the Battle of the Ice, Nevsky found himself amnesiac surrounded by worshippers. Though in the twenty years since, Nevsky has regained his memory and returned to Novagrad, his flock has followed him, making Novagrad a key pilgrimage point for followers of the Cult of Wodin

Organizational Structure

Religious proceedings rely heavily upon story telling, relating tales of Wodin and his allies and reveling in the lifestyles of those stories, which focus heavily upon battle and celebration. The organization itself is more a loose grouping of storytellers in each tribe, who share tales with each other. There are few cults that have raised the religion to a truly structured form. Two groups of note are: The Cult of Thuris settled in the north, along the coast of the Thuris Fjord, named after Wodin's son and blacksmith who supposedly hammered out the Fjords to provide natural docks to Wodin's boats; The Cult of Nevsky, situated in the city of Novagrad, as near as tolerable to their religious icon.

Religious Iconography

Wodin - The ideal Hamster, fierce in combat, festive in celebration. Theologists believe there may have been a real hamster who became idolized into the modern Wodin, some scholars suggest this original 'Wodin' may have lead the Hamsters down out of the north to smite the Rodentian Empire. This 'real Wodin' theory is panned by the majority of researchers, as hamster tales are often exaggerated or out-right lies, used to bolster their image as horrific barbarians.

Lokke - The wolf trickster represents in modern Wodinism the threat of 'intelligence' and 'civilization'. As a pejorative, the name is used as an explicative or to describe traitors to the tribe. As Wodinists idolize the ideal of fearlessness, Lokke is never seen as a demonic threatening figure, nor as a villain to be actively destroyed. Although Lokke is often interpreted as a wolf, Hamsters have never seen the Ursal wolves as a threat, or nemesis. Researchers generally accept that this syncs well with Lokke rarely taking on an evil aspect in the tales he appears, only a comedic element, or annoyance.

Trolls and Trollhunters - Horrid creatures from beyond time, that gnaw at the world tree. Trolls are monstrous creatures from beneath the earth. Trollhunters are the foolhardy Wodinists that go seeking their destruction. Though they are rarely hunted for a cause beyond another tale to tell and trophies to show off, some Wodinists see Trolls and their worshippers as a threat to the world and devote themselves to trollhunting.

The Shadows - The flying shadows, spoken of throughout the Sagas of Wodin, have no proper names within the written copies of the tales. They are often seen as a guiding hand to Wodin and to all Wodinists. The Shadows appear in several situations to save the life of Wodin or his followers and eventually guided him to sack the southern kingdoms and to his final journey to the east. Modern scholars who follow the 'real Wodin' theory believe these shadows may have been remnants of the Avian kingdoms but no archaeological evidence suggests Sapient birds have ever travelled so far north. As the northern areas of the Vandalands are dark for many months of the winter, darkness is not seen as an evil omen or menace. The torch being a key feature of Vandal combat for centuries, illumination was not difficult to obtain when raiding.

Ranks

Lay (Recruit)

Requirements - Any person who has heard a saga of Wodin or his kin, that revels in combat and celebration can consider themselves a Lay Wodinist.

Saga-Teller (Private)

Requirements - After memorizing at least 3 Sagas and gaining 30% in 4 Organizational Skills and dedicating 1 POW to their Duty(Wodinism), a Wodinist becomes a Saga-Teller, who can readily share stories with others and show what is best in life.

Rewards - After travelling to a cult's shrine and proving your knowledge of Wodin through the retelling of 3 Sagas. A personal Hamster Great Axe is forged for the Saga-Teller, this weapon is both a real weapon and an instrument in retelling stories, letting the Saga-Teller swing the weapon about while retelling epic battles.

Compulsions - During downtime, usually around a campfire, the Saga-Teller must share stories, or learn new ones from their companions. The more alcohol and general revelry involved the better.

Shaman (Sergeant)

Requirements - After memorizing at least 5 Sagas and gaining 50% in 4 Organizational Skills and dedicated at least 3 POW to their Duty (Wodinism), the Saga-Teller can return to a cult's shrine and defeat in single combat (not to the death) a Wodinist of Shaman rank or higher to become a Shaman themselves.

Rewards - With the completion of a trial by combat, a second Hamster Great Axe is forged for the Shaman. Wodin was renowned for his dual axe Combat Style and this second axe represents a Shaman's devotion to the ways of Wodin.

Compulsions - Saga-telling must continue to be a part of the Shaman's life, learning and sharing new stories. The Shaman must also begin training to dual wield two-handed weapons, specifically the Hamster Great Axes.

War Shaman (Officer)

Requirements - After reaching at least 80% Skill in Dual Great Axe Combat Style, learning 8 Sagas and dedicating at least 4 POW, the Shaman may take another trial by combat, facing two War Shamans. Combat ends when one War Shaman is slain, or the Adventurer is slain.

Rewards - The final saga of Wodin, The Gotterdammerung is shared with the War Shaman, detailing the return of Wodin and the end of the world. This tale is not to be shared with anyone below War Shaman rank.

Compulsions - Continue to learn new stories and maintain skill with their Great Axes. Must participate in Trial by combat against rising Shamans and never share the final saga with others.

High Shaman (Commander)

Requirements - When a High Shaman is dying he selects his successor from the War Shamans of his cult. If the High Shaman dies before naming a successor, the War Shamans fight for the position in a melee, each candidate fighting alone against the others. The last standing War Shaman wins leadership.

Rewards - Command of the entire cult, able to direct raiding parties and determine the eligibility of others to increase their rank.

Compulsions - Always lead your followers in the ways of Wodin: Combat and Celebration. Never forget the sagas of Wodin and readily share them with others, except for the final saga, which will be shared with the world when Wodin returns and Ragnarok begins.

Organization Skills

Brawn, Dance, Sing, Oratory, Play Instrument, Lore(Wodinism), 2H Axe Combat Style, Dual 2H Axe Combat Style.

Lore (Wodinism) - Every 10% skill represents an additional Saga the Wodinist has learned. Additional Sagas can also be learned from ancient Wodinist Ruins, or from stories shared by others. Only Wodinist Sagas count toward the number of Sagas as required for promotion.

Current Divisions and Commanders

Cult of Thuris - A Cult that worships Thuris, the son of Wodin, the first of the Trollhunters. Followers of this cult may also learn 2H Hammer or Dual 2H Hammer combat styles, Dual 2H Hammer can replace the Dual 2H Axe skill requirement for War Shaman. They are based out of the Hamster city of Thrudvangr nestled in the northern Fjords.

Hans Jespersen - High Shaman of the Cult of Thuris, this hamster is rather young for his current position but is popular for his conservative views, encouraging Wodinists to follow the path of a Trollhunter, creating one's own tales to expand the religion.

Cult of Nevsky - A Cult that believes Wodin has returned in the body of Arctos Nevsky, the bear Prince of Novagrad. They are based out of the city of Novagrad, trying to be as close to their object of worship as possible.

Asatru Wanes - One of the hamsters that discovered Nevsky after the Battle of the Ice, Asatru founded this version of the cult in the weeks during Nevsky's recovery. Asatru Wanes now finds the cult losing its population as Nevsky has regained his memories and continues to refute his 'god-hood'.

Common Missions/Plot Threads

Ale Raid - Alcohol is a key feature of Wodinist celebrations and storytelling. When the ale runs low, Wodinists often go forth and raid local villages for beer. This may come in the form of actual raids, pillaging the towns and stealing their liquor, or simply 'invading' the local tavern, taking up more tables then necessary and carrying on into the late hours with stories and boisterous laughter.

Actual Raids - Combat is one of the ideals of Wodin and perfecting oneself with the whirling of axes, brings a worshipper that much closer to Wodin. Strategy is of little concern to Wodinists, they simply pick a target and smite it and then return home sharing the story with others. High Shamans may sometimes send others out on challenges, picking a particularly formidable opponent, such as a single bear or wolf of the Ursal Khanate, or an entire fortress of the Bubonic Knights. The exact makeup of a raiding party can vary from a single hamster, to an entire tribe, it just depends on the whims of the Wodinists.

Pilgrimage - Each cult has a focal point of their beliefs, these may take the form of ancient shrines, or major landmarks. For Thuris Wodinists, the Thuris Fjord is a common pilgrimage point, while for Nevsky Wodinists, attempting to catch sight of the Bear Prince in Novagrad is a mission all its own. In any case, once arriving at the pilgrimage site, Wodinists will perform their usual activities, until a new story comes to them to share upon their return.

CAMPAIGNS

This section provides a Game Master with a few ideas for basic genres of campaigns to play in *Historia Rodentia*. Paired with the Missions/Plot Threads from the organizations your players join, you can easily craft a campaign that is relevant to each player. Everything below is merely a suggestion of how to get a campaign started and not actual rules.

Types of Campaigns

War Campaigns

War is an ever present threat in the 19th Century. One might even say that war never changes. With armies posturing across a field, heroes must guide their nation to victory, or be overwhelmed by the oncoming hordes. Playing a campaign like this usually requires Adventurers to be from one or two nations at most to keep players on the same side of the war.

Political Campaigns

Even when their soldiers are not on the battlefield, nations are still at war, only on the political stage. The machinations of back room dealings can change the world as much as any battle. Of course, choosing sides is the first step and this can easily place players in opposite corners.

Exploration Campaigns

Colonialism is past its peak but there are still places in the world to be found or explored. Adventurers can set sail with a crew and find what is out there, visit foreign lands or colonies of their home nations. Their vessel of choice could be a sailing ship or even a prototype airship or submarine, created by one of the technology firms.

Horror Campaigns

There are horrible ancient things below the earth. Insects, or Exomorphs to the people of *Historia Rodentia*, have slumbering hives and megacolonies that spread across the planet. Modern industry is beginning to run into these creatures again and few are prepared to fight their massive numbers, or their horrific leaders.

Classical Campaigns

Sometimes an army or government is too grand a setting and a classic 'dungeon run' is a great way to break up the pace. Some bandits may have settled in an abandoned castle, or pirates have stolen a noble's daughter. Either way, a small band of Adventurers are the perfect option for solving these problems.

Using Miniatures in *Historia Rodentia*

In some situations, it is beneficial to have a visual representation of where party members are located, mainly in combat. Miniatures help give you visual guidance about who is where in a situation and should be considered abstract rather then definitive. We recommend having the GM draw out the frame work of where a combat is taking place (such as a building or streets) and place miniatures down to show where players and NPCs are located it. Combat and movement still follow the standard rules. This is more for the benefit of players remembering where they are located and what they are fighting.

Exonomicon

Ignore the Bestiary section of the *Legend Core Rulebook*. The following pages detail the horrible creatures you might encounter in Eutheria.

Exomorphs

The slumbering empire of the exomorphs is once again on the rise. A relic of an ancient age, these carapaced, exoskeletal creatures share no commonality with Eutherians or Reptilians. These creatures are of one mind and it seeks to wipe all other life from the surface of the world. Diplomacy will get you nowhere with most members of this 'species' as their minds are not made for decision making. Only the rare few 'royal' ranks of the Exomorphs can even coerce their underlings to mimic Eutherian speech. With a sapient mind to focus them, Exomorphs can, working in concert, form a collective speech pattern, able to weave their chittering together into a horrible voice. Even if such a situation was to arise, the sapient exomorph would be more likely to tell you of your coming doom, then open discussion.

Will O'Wisp - Firefly Exomorph

Those that are searching for exomorph hives often know their location by the Will O'Wisps that float about near tunnel entrances. These tiny exomorphs buzz about emitting light as a warning system. The unprepared should run before Legion exomorphs burst from below to attack the invaders.

Legion - Ant Exomorph

	Dice	Average			1D20	Hit Location	AP/HP
STR	2D6	7			1	Right Rear Leg	2/4
CON	2D6+4	12			2	Left Rear Leg	2/4
SIZ	2D4	5	Tiny		3	Right Middle Leg	2/4
INT	2	2			4	Left Middle Leg	2/4
DEX	2D6+4	12			5-9	Abdomen	2/6
					10-13	Thorax	2/7
					14	Right Front Leg	2/4
Combat Actions	2				15	Left Front Leg	2/4
Damage Modifier	-1D4				16-20	Head	2/5
Movement	12m						
Strike Rank	+7						

Typical Armor: Chitin Carapace (2AP) No Armor penalty
Traits: Hive Mind, Wall Walking, Formidable Natural Weapons
Skills: Athletics 75%, Evade 40%, Perception 30%, Persistence 50%, Resilience 60%, Stealth 25%, Track 85%

Combat Styles

Mandibles 40%, Sting 45%

Weapons

Type	Size	Reach	Damage	AP/HP
Mandibles	M	M	1D8-1D4	As for Head
Sting	S	T	1D6+Acid	As for Thorax

Hive Mind

Legion exomorphs are, as their name implies, a collective. Each additional member of the legion provides +1 INT to the total group when they are working in tandem to perform a task. For example, a group of three Legion attacking the Adventurers have 4 INT (2 base, plus 2 for the extra two legion). This affects their Strike Rank and Combat Actions. A Hive Mind can be disrupted if a member of the group is killed. The slayer should make a Heroic Command roll against the Legion's Persistence to attempt to disrupt this ability. If successful, the INT value reverts to 2 and all members gain a level of fatigue (maximum one level from this effect). Hive Mind cannot be restored until combat is over.

Sting

This secondary attack can only be used after performing the Grip Combat Manoeuvre with its mandibles. The Sting applies Strong acid in addition to the normal damage it deals. Immediately after succeeding a Grip Manoeuvre.

Creature Notes

Legion work with a swarm mentality, where each member is rarely effective, enough bodies can move mountains. Legion make up the bulk of the exomorph hive, performing duties as workers and soldiers. Most encounters with exomorphs are with these swarming monsters. In combat, Legion swarm their opponents, attempting to overwhelm them with sheer numbers. Generally these should be seen as underlings, or with General HP, rarely should they be fought as a singular threat.

Troll - Large Beetle Exomorph

	Dice	Average		1D20	Hit Location	AP/HP
STR	2D6+12	19		1	Right Rear Leg	5/7
CON	2D6+12	19		2	Left Rear Leg	5/7
SIZ	1D6+12	15	Large	3	Right Middle Leg	5/7
INT	2	2		4	Left Middle Leg	5/7
DEX	1D6+6	10		5-9	Abdomen	5/8
				10-13	Thorax	5/9
				14	Right Front Leg	5/7
				15	Left Front Leg	5/7
Combat Actions		2		16-20	Head	5/7
Damage Modifier		+1D4				
Movement		5m				
Strike Rank		+6				

Typical Armor: Chitin Carapace (5 AP), no Armor Penalty.
Traits: Formidable Natural Weapons
Skills: Brawn 75%, Athletics 40%, Evade 20%, Perception 50%, Persistence 35%, Resilience 60%, Track 40%

Combat Styles
Mandibles 50%

Weapons

Type	Size	Reach	Damage	AP/HP
Mandibles	M	M	1D8+1D4	As for Head

Jotnar - Huge Beetle Exomorph

	Dice	Average		1D20	Hit Location	AP/HP
STR	4D6+12	26		1	Right Rear Leg	6/10
CON	4D6+12	26		2	Left Rear Leg	6/10
SIZ	1D6+20	24	Huge	3	Right Middle Leg	6/10
INT	2	2		4	Left Middle Leg	6/10
DEX	1D6+6	10		5-9	Abdomen	6/11
				10-13	Thorax	6/12
				14	Right Front Leg	6/10
Combat Actions		1		15	Left Front Leg	6/10
Damage Modifier		+1D10		16-20	Head	6/10
Movement		8m				
Strike Rank		+6				

Typical Armor: Chitin Carapace (6AP), no Armor Penalty.
Traits: Formidable Natural Weapons
Skills: Brawn 100%, Athletics 35%, Evade 20%, Perception 40%, Persistence 35%, Resilience 70%, Track 40%

Combat Styles
Mandibles 50%

Weapons

Type	Size	Reach	Damage	AP/HP
Mandibles	M	M	1D8+1D10	As for Head

Creature Notes

One of the few Exomorphs that travel above ground, tales of Trolls and Jotnar go back for centuries. These creatures, legend has it, emerge from their caves to feed, crushing and destroying anything in their path to a source of food. Every now and then, a farmer will find his fences crushed, his crops uprooted and his steeds torn apart and fed upon but he will swear he heard a storm batter his lands. In combat, the Trolls and Jotnar use their bulk to charge through obstacles and crushing their prey before feasting on it.

Pazuzu - Wasp Exomorph

	Dice	Average		1D20	Hit Location	AP/HP
STR	4D6	14		1	Right Rear Leg	3/4
CON	2D6	9		2	Left Rear Leg	3/4
SIZ	1D6+6	10	Tiny	3	Right Middle Leg	3/4
INT	2	2		4	Left Middle Leg	3/4
DEX	2D6+6	13		5-7	Abdomen	3/5
				8-9	Thorax	3/6
				10-11	Right Wing	1/4
Combat Actions		2		12-13	Left Wing	1/4
Damage Modifier		+0		14	Right Front Leg	3/4
Movement		12m		15	Left Front Leg	3/4
Strike Rank		+8		16-20	Head	3/4

Traits: Hive Mind, Flying, Wall Walking, Venomous Sting
Typical Armor: Chitin Carapace (3 AP). No Armor Penalty
Skills: Athletics 70%, Evade 50%, Perception 40%, Persistence 45%, Resilience 45%, Track 50%

Combat Styles
Sting 40%, Small Maw 45%

Weapons

Type	Size	Reach	Damage	AP/HP
Small Maw	M	T	1D4	As for Head
Sting	S	T	1D4+1	As for Abdomen

Hive Mind
As the Legion Hive Mind Trait.

Venomous Sting
Application: Injected by Sting Attack
Onset time: 1D12 Combat Rounds
Duration: 6D10 minutes
Resistance Time: The victim must make a Resistance roll at the Onset Time. Failure indicates that Condition has taken effect
Potency: CON x5 + CON per additional sting.
Resistance: Resilience.
Conditions: Agony. The venom initially causes the victim pain if the first Resistance roll is failed. Even if the Roll is succeeded, further Stings increase the potency, track the 'duration' of the venom until it wears off. Antidote/Cure: Antivenom.

Creature Notes

In ancient myths, Pazuzu were the demons of the sky, covering the sun and hearkening the oncoming hordes. In the Rodeniad, the Avians focused their war on these flying monsters, the only Exomorphs that could reach their strongholds. Rare is the flying monster in modern times but in places far from civilization, travelers tell of their fellow wanderers being picked up from the trail by roaming shadows. In combat, Pazuzu use their sting to cripple their opponents and then often grapple them, carrying them off to their hives.

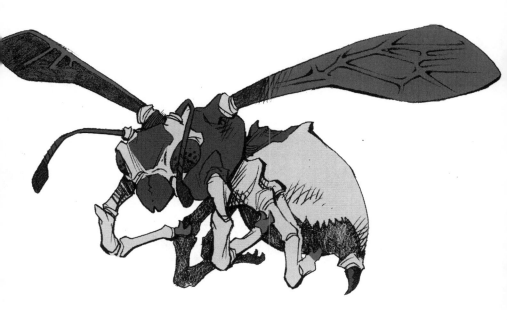

Diabolos - Mantis Exomorph

	Dice	Average		1D20	Hit Location	AP/HP
STR	3D6	11		1	Right Rear Leg	3/5
CON	3D6	11		2	Left Rear Leg	3/5
SIZ	1D6+16	20	Very Large	3-5	Abdomen	3/6
INT	3D6+4	15		6	Right Wing	3/5
POW	3D6	9		7	Left Wing	3/5
DEX	2D6+18	25		8	Right Front Leg	3/5
				9	Left Front Leg	3/5
Combat Actions		3		10-12	Thorax	3/7
Damage Modifier		+0		13-15	Right Claw	3/4
Tactical Points		20		16-18	Left Claw	3/4
Movement		12m		19-20	Head	3/5
Strike Rank		+20				

Typical Armor: Chitin Carapace (3 AP), no Armor Penalty.
Traits: Formidable Natural Weapons, Wall Walking, Hive Leader, Fleet
Tactical Abilities: Striking Leap I, Furious Maul, Faith I, Faith II, Just as Planned
Skills: Athletics 75%, Evade 50%, Perception 85%, Persistence 45%, Resilience 70%, Stealth 50%, Track 35%, Heroic Command 40%, Battlefield Awareness 40%, Language (Any) 50%, Lore (Exomorphism) 100%, Duty (Exomorphism) 80%
Organization: Exomorphism (Officer)

Combat Styles
Claw 75%, Small Maw 60%

Weapons

Type	Size	Reach	Damage	AP/HP
Small Maw	M	T	1D8	As for Head
Claw	L	VL	1D10	As for Right Claw
Claw	L	VL	1D10	As for Left Claw

Hive Leader
The sapient leaders of the exomorphs are able to augment their Hive Mind followers. Any creatures with Hive Mind have a base +5 INT as long as their Hive Mind rule is not interrupted. This ability overrides another creature's Hive Commander Trait and does not stack with Hive Commanders or other Hive Leaders

Chittering Madness
Although Exomorphs may know languages, their physiology does not allow them to make the same sounds as Mammals or Reptiles. The only way they can 'speak' is by chorus, forcing a

variety of exomorphs to each make the appropriate noise to mimic the speech of a single creature. Such choruses are not a common occurrence when encountering Exomorphs but can be arranged in extreme circumstances. The sound of such choruses is also depressing and horrifying to those that hear it. Listeners must make a Persistence check to resist a level of fatigue.

Creature Notes

One of the leading species of the Exomorphs, Mantids are highly intelligent and incredibly cunning. Although they would prefer to let their legions of minions slaughter their foes, they are formidable opponents in combat. Using their unnatural speed, they leap upon their foes and, using their scythe-like forearms, slash repeatedly until their foe stops moving. They will then continue in a sort of feral rage destroying their opponents until they are the only creature left standing. They then compose themselves and leave massacre scene.

Mephistophilis - Spider Exomorph

	Dice	Average		1D20	Hit Location	AP/HP
STR	1D6+6	10		1	Right Fourth Leg	4/7
CON	3D6+4	15		2	Left Fourth Leg	4/7
SIZ	1D6+16	20	Very Large	3	Right Third Leg	4/7
INT	3D6+4	15		4	Left Third Leg	4/7
POW	3D6	9		5-11	Abdomen	4/12
DEX	2D6+18	25		12	Right Second Leg	4/7
				13	Left Second Leg	4/7
				14	Right First Leg	4/7
				15	Left First Leg	4/7
Combat Actions		3		16-20	Thorax	4/11
Damage Modifier		+1D2				
Tactical Points		20				
Movement		12m				
Strike Rank		+20				

Typical Armor: Chitin Carapace (4 AP), No armor penalty
Traits: Venomous Bite, Wall Walking, Hive Commander
Tactical Abilities: Striking Leap I, Faith I, Faith II, Just as Planned
Skills: Athletics 110%, Evade 40%, Perception 65%, Persistence 50%, Resilience 60%, Stealth 85%, Track 40%, First Aid 30%, Healing 30%, Lore (Exomorphism) 100%, Duty (Exomorphism) 80%
Organization: Exomorphism (Officer)

Combat Styles
Bite 60%, Unarmed 75%, Web 30%

Weapons

Type	SIZ	Reach	Damage	AP/HP
Bite	M	T	1D6+1D2	As for Head
Unarmed	L	VL	1D10	As for Right First Leg
Unarmed	L	VL	1D10	As for Left First Leg
Web	L	L	Entangles	4/10

Venomous Bite
Application: Injected by Bite Attack
Onset time: 1D3 Rounds.
Duration: 1D3 Days.
Resistance Time: Daily. The first Resistance roll must be made at the end of the Onset Time, then daily thereafter. Successfully resisting the poison allows the victim to avoid suffering the conditions until the next roll must be made.
Potency: 40+ CON of Spider.
Resistance: Resilience.
Conditions: Paralysis.
Antidote/Cure: Healing skill with Antivenom.

Web

The web is incredibly strong. All webs have 4 AP but the strength of the web in Hit Points is equal to the spider's own STR. Those caught in the web suffer the effects of the Entangle Combat Manoeuvre, across 1D3 separate locations at the same time. If a victim is able to move across the web, his movement is reduced by two thirds.

Hive Commander

Able to give basic commands to the Hive Mind exomorphs, a Hive Commander gives a +3 INT bonus to Hive Mind exomorphs within 20m of it. This Trait is overridden by Hive Leader and does not stack with other Hive Commanders.

Chittering Madness

As the Diabolos Chittering Madness Trait

Creature Notes

A horrible cross between a torturer and a scientist, the rare Mephistophilis exomorph steals victims in the dead of the night, having paralyzed them with its venom. Such victims are only seen again in the deep forests, dancing like marionettes, luring fellow villagers to their doom. Rumors also say, those, who have sold their souls to the Exomorphs, are contacted by Mephistophilis exomorphs, who carry them away, or share their secrets. In combat this Exomorph lays webbing across openings as traps, to slow down opponents so it can paralyze them with its venom.

Black Queen - Ant Queen Exomorph

	Dice	Average		1D20	Hit Location	AP/HP
STR	2D6	7		1	Right Rear Leg	5/7
CON	2D6+4	11		2	Left Rear Leg	5/7
SIZ	1D8+16	21	Very Large	3	Right Middle Leg	5/7
INT	3D6+4	15		4	Left Middle Leg	5/7
POW	3D6+4	15		5-9	Abdomen	5/8
DEX	1D6+4	8		10-13	Thorax	5/9
				14	Right Front Leg	5/7
Combat Actions		4		15	Left Front Leg	5/7
Damage Modifier		+1D2		16-20	Head	5/7
Tactical Points		12				
Movement		4m				
Strike Rank		+12				

Typical Armor: Chitin Carapace (5AP), No Armor penalty
Traits: March of the Black Queen, Formidable Natural Weapons, Chittering Madness
Tactical Abilities: Faith I, Faith II, Just as Planned
Skills: Athletics 75%, Evade 40%, Perception 30%, Persistence 50%, Resilience 60%, Stealth 25%, Track 85%, Lore (Exomorphism) 100%, Duty (Exomorphism) 100%
Organization: Exomorphism (Commander)

Combat Styles
Mandibles 40%

Weapons

Type	Size	Reach	Damage	AP/HP
Mandibles	M	M	1D8+1D2	As for Head

March of the Black Queen

The minions of the Black Queen number in the billions and when she calls, they come to her side. As a Combat Action, the Black Queen can summon 1D3+1 Legion from nearby tunnels, caves, or soft earth. If any of these areas are not nearby, the Legion must travel from the nearest tunnel, cave or soft earth to reach her. Any Legion that answer her call have +3 INT which stacks with Hive Commander or Hive Leader. As an alternative use of this ability, she can forgo summoning additional Legion to give an additional Combat Action to each Legion already in combat.

Chittering Madness

As the Diabolos Chittering Madness Trait

Creature Notes

The supreme leaders of the Exomorphs, the Black Queens are near immortal, with their identical spawn seeded throughout the world, ready to hatch upon their death. Secreted away in a safe section of the hive, the Black Queens constantly spawn new hellish minions. This eternal pregnancy leaves them nearly defenseless and as such, their honor guard of male Legion (regular HP rather than general or underling) are always prepared to give their lives for their queens. In combat, the Queen will attempt to keep her distance and continually call for her minions to protect her.

Index

Many thanks to Matthew Sprange and Mongoose Publishing for making this book possible.